# MEET THE 'STANS

Printed in United Kingdom
Hertfordshire Press Ltd © 2020
e-mail: publisher@hertfordshirepress.com
www.hertfordshirepress.com

Christopher Jones ©
**MEET THE 'STANS**
**Getting Lost In History**

English

Book Designer Ivica Jandrijevic

Cover photo used under license from Shutterstock.
Interior images by Library of Congress, Wikipedia

All other images taken and owned by the author.

*British Library Catalogue in Publication Data
A catalogue record for this book is available from the British Library
Library of Congress in Publication Data
A catalogue record for this book has been requested*

Printed in Turkey by Elma Basım
**ISBN: 978-1-913356-15-6**

# CHRISTOPHER JONES

# MEET
# THE 'STANS

## GETTING LOST IN HISTORY

HERTFORDSHIRE PRESS

# CONTENTS

# PROLOGUE

Your travels through Russia look amazing!" a less than erudite friend had messaged me as I was taking off from Bishkek, capital of Kyrgyzstan. Having only ever been to Russia briefly two years prior, I thought this message quite nicely exemplified the reason I had boarded this—by EU Standards—dangerous flight, and had been making my way through Central Asia for the past few months. Not just for the endless conversations that I could one day punctuate with a contrived look of smug amazement followed by "Dushanbe, you haven't been?" but also because I felt I was exploring an unexplored part of the world. Of course, not in the literal sense. If anything, it was extremely well-explored. Alexander the Great, Marco Polo, Genghis Khan, Stalin and numerous other historic figures had all cut their teeth here. But it was unexplored in the sense that it was absent from any Sunday newspaper travel section, was still spared from marching bands of retirees and hadn't yet been graced by those lovely stag parties you see quietly contemplating the museums and galleries throughout Europe. Though perhaps this wasn't without reason. This is not a region where you're welcomed with a lei placed around your neck and handed a cold drink. More likely, your plane will glide down to a smog covered Central Asian city of your choice, the passengers will all break into applause, you'll be squeezed out like a tube of toothpaste with the other passengers pushing and shoving from the plane and into the seat of a 40-year-old Lada, narrowly avoid a couple of head-on collisions before paying your grinning gold-toothed driver ten times the local rate. But of course, that's all part of the fun.

And the reason it's part of the fun is because the traveller who finds themself here is not here for comfort. Instead, that traveller is in Central Asia to see what life in the USSR was like, to hike mountain ranges that extend eight kilometres into the sky, to walk through cities that the armies of Alexander the Great had built and Genghis Khan's Golden Horde had destroyed. To absorb in the Registan of Samarkand without another tourist, to witness the extraordinarily beautiful women of Kazakhstan and Kyrgyzstan and extraordinarily disagreeable women of Uzbekistan. To eat horse and shun pork, to join pilgrims at ancient sacred sites and ultimately to remove themself from comfort for something raw, authentic, interesting and fun.

I should point out though that perhaps unlike others, I was shielded slightly when it came to negative experiences.

The idea to write this book germinated early in my trip, and because of that, each time I played Central Asian roulette with my underwear, exposed myself to radiation or ate chunks of horse fat covered in a couple of dozen flies having an orgy, I was able to say to myself, 'Well, at least it'll be good for the book.'

# ONCE UPON A TIME
# IN CENTRAL ASIA

Answering "Central Asia" to the question of where you've been for two months does not serve language's purpose of transferring knowledge between individuals. This would often be illustrated by the follow-up response which—in my experience at least—constituted "Beautiful!", "Lucky you" and "Wow, did you party much?" Now... sure... all of these responses could arguably be legitimate reflections of these people's understanding of where I'd been. A friend may have been referring to the Pamir mountain ranges above Bishkek when she exclaimed "Beautiful!", another, the night-life of Almaty when they asked about the partying. "Lucky you" is a little more tricky. But perhaps they were referring to the experience of walking amongst the splendour of Samarkand without encountering another tourist. In saying that, this friend would have a hard time finding Belgium on a map so he may have just been having a stab in the dark. Which is barely his fault however as Central Asia remains largely absent from most tourist maps.

*    *    *    *

With a total population of 70 or so million people, the five countries of this region are visited by roughly 5.5 million people annually. Compare this with, say France which has a population of 67 million yet is visited by 83 million people a year, or better yet, Spain, with only a population of 47 million but receives a whopping 75 million tourists annually. Central Asia is not a place where residents are demanding the regulation of Airbnb. It should be said though, that these number are total and that naughty 'stan in the South—Turkmenistan (population 6 million), receives a grand total of 8,000 people a year—slightly more than Libya but almost half that of Afghanistan. "Ha ha, you are a very strange man!" the manager of my hotel in Ashgabat, capital of Turkmenistan, had responded after I told him I was there as a tourist. While the region is somewhat invisible to the modern traveller and indeed to the modern world, this was not always the case. Like a perspective painting where everything close is large and everything far is small, the last two centuries of European dominance seem almost immutable. But as we enter the third decade of this $21^{st}$ century, the centre of geopolitical gravity is steadily shifting back to Asia, where for a large part of human history it once had sat. And it was often the actors and events that played out in Central Asia that were responsible for anchoring it there. Though to tell the history of the region, it's worth starting with a very European figure. And a figure who like many of those who crashed their way through the region, saw himself (it was always a man) as God's gift to humanity if not an actual god.

*    *    *    *

"I hold the Earth", runs the inscription beneath a statue of Alexander the Great, "and you Zeus, hold Olympus". Born in 356 BC to King Phillip II and into his expanding $4^{th}$ Century BC Kingdom of Macedonia, privately educated by Aristotle, and successfully commanding Greek armies by the age of 16, Alexander the Great was the pinnacle of self-confidence. That his mother perpetuated the rumour that she had been impregnated by Zeus undoubtedly helped. At the age of twenty, and following the assassination of the King, Alexander ascended to the throne and almost immediately set about expanding his Empire. To the east lay the Empire of Persia—at the time the largest empire to have ever existed—an empire that had been harassing the ancient Greeks for centuries and an empire that Alexander declared he would bring down. And a mere five years later, in 331 BC, and after three years of almost continuous battles occurring ever deeper in Persian territory, Alexander led an army of 47,000 in what is now northern Iraq and defeated King Darius III of Persia and his army of 105,000. Having brought the largest empire ever known to its knees, from which it was not to recover for another century, rather than returning home, Alexander the Great pressed on.

*From the West comes change…*

"Bucephalus drank from this spring", my guide had said to me, as we were both crouched over, lapping up the crystal-clear water in our hands from a spring high up in the mountains above Dushanbe, capital of Tajikistan. He had been referring to Alexander the Great's famous horse and was saying it while I looked up at him nodding enthusiastically, internally knowing too well that he was almost certainly making this up on the spot. Yet as it happened, I was being blinded by my own arrogance as Alexander the Great *had* indeed ridden through this way and past the lake that now bore his name—Lake Iskanderkul.* And thinking back, a natural spring bubbling pristine fresh water hardly seemed an unlikely spot for a horse to lap from.

*       *       *       *

Alexander's army had marched through here 2,300 years earlier on his way into India, having just established the city of Alexandra Eschate ('Alexandra the Furthest') 170 km to the north. Today that city, Tajikistan's second largest, is known as Khujand, though was once called Leninbad following the arrival of a different set of foreign imperialists a couple of thousand years after the first. And 230 km to

---

* 'Iskander' meaning Alexander in Persia, 'kul' meaning lake in Turkik.

the south he established Alexanderia-Oxiana ('Alexandria on the Oxus' in reference to the Oxus river), today sitting in Uzbekistan and known as Termez, and a city which too felt the impact of a foreign power when in 2003 the United States used it as a staging post into Afghanistan. These were but two of the nine cities he established in Central Asia, all of which he named after himself, marking his route through the region. Each was built to Greek standards and often included Greek gymnasiums, theatres, city squares, and grid street systems. And they were reinforced by leaving behind a few thousand Greek infantrymen who were expected to marry local girls and live out the rest of their lives in this newly expanded part of the Macedonian Empire. While some of them were overrun and destroyed in the ensuing millennia, the lasting impact of the tens of thousands of Europeans he left in the region remained. A fact that I would often encounter while in Central Asia when I would find myself struck by the features of a European, otherwise entirely out of place*.

By 323 BC though he had returned home, and only a few years after his rampage through Central Asia, at the age of thirty-two Alexander the Great died**. In what became

---

\* While not strictly Central Asia, for readers interested in seeing what Europeans looking out of place looks like, search Google images for 'Kalash People'. A group of people descended from Alexander the Great's army who today live in the northern mountains of Pakistan.

\*\* How he died is not conclusive, though it was either from drinking himself to death, typhoid or being poisoned.

known as the Partition of Triparadisus, his Empire was split between his generals with the Central Asia portion of his empire going to his infantry general Seleceus I Nictator, whose reign established the Seleucid Empire. Within 70 years, however, this Empire broke apart and the area covering part of modern Kazakhstan, Turkmenistan, Tajikistan, and Uzbekistan came to be known as the Greco-Bactrian Kingdom. This was very much a Greek Kingdom that retained its Greek Culture and links with its Mediterranean forebears. For the century and a half the kingdom existed, it produced coins, pottery, and sculpture—all in the Greek style and script. Though as time progressed, interaction with the Indian sub-continent to the south increased leading to new styles and new ideas. By the later parts of the kingdom's history, coins began appearing that looked for the most part Greek except that on one side would appear the multiple arms of an Indian God. With this interaction

2nd Century BC  came the shifting south of the kingdom's centre of gravity, and as the Greco-Bactria kingdom began to dissolve, the Indo-Greek began to rise. This new kingdom, however, was short-lived. What had been like a soft flame of Greek culture was slowly extinguished as nomadic peoples of the north began encroaching on the region, displacing those long-held Greek styles with their own. And with the rise of the Indo-Scythians who came to control most of southern Central Asia and the Kushan Empire who took the northern part, Greek-influence in the region finally came to an end'. All the while this demographic and political change was occurring in Central Asia, to the East and the West of the region were rising two new Empires, both of which were to have a significant and lasting impact on the region and indeed the world. To the East rose the Han Dynasty which came to represent a golden age in Chinese history and to the West the Empire of Rome.

*From trade comes wealth…*

With the rise of these empires came a leap in both the con- 0-500 AD sumption and production of sophisticated goods and an explosion in international trade. Under the Han Dynasty, formal trading routes were established towards the West, while road building under the Roman Empire, pushed their network East. Trade began to flow across these now overlapping routes, and for the first time in history, consumers at one end of the world were suddenly connected on a mass scale with producers at the other. Goods were transported by merchants and their pack animals, which generally meant double-humped Bactrian camels, able to carry up to 250 kg each at a pace of almost 50 km a day. In what became known as caravans, these merchants would travel in groups, linking their camels together by connecting chains from the tail of one camel to the perforated nose of the next**. The cities and

---

\* It's worth noting that Greek pottery was still appearing in Samarkand hundreds of years later.

\*\* Armin Vambery in his book Travels in Central Asia mentions the dreadful suffering of the animals when one camel was to suddenly stop.

towns along these routes adapted to accommodate their needs and established formal way stations known as Caravanserais.

This trade was so marked that a 19th century German Geographer named it after the silk that flowed from China to Europe. He came to call it Seidenstraße, or in English— the Silk Road. The produce travelling the Silk Road would often come from such faraway places that by the time they found their final buyer they would often be shrouded in myth and conjecture. Take for instance this excerpt from Peter Hopkirk's excellent book *The Great Game:*

> *The Romans did not know the land the silks came from. Somewhere edging the easternmost sea, they heard, the country of the Seres escaped influence of the stars, and was guided only by the laws of its ancestors. Mars never drove its people to war, nor Venus to folly. They had no temples, no prostitutes, no crimes, no victims. The king's women – seven hundred of them – rode in golden chariots drawn by oxen. But this land of Serica, by some divine spell, was impossible to read. Meanwhile the Chinese, in mirror image, came to believe that in a great city to the west – Rome, Alexandria or Constantinople – the people were ruled by Philosophers, peacefully elected. Their palaces rose on crystal pillars, and they travelled in little white draped carriages, and signalled their movements by the shaking of bells.*

A very romantic vision of what lay beyond the horizon by both sides, especially the Romans who if you go by the nightclubs of Uzbekistan, got it marginally wrong about the prostitutes.

This opening up of markets and explosion in trade massively enriched the cities that it passed through, and with Central Asia located between these two empires, this region hugely benefited. Cities never before seen in such size began appearing in the region, many becoming enormously rich. Merv for instance, a city in today's Turkmenistan, exploded in size which by the 12th century made it the largest and richest on Earth, earning it the name at the time of the 'Queen of the World'. Or Nishpur, though now in Iran, was during the era of the Silk Road a major city in a major Central Asia Empire and at the turn of the first millennium AD had a population four times that of then London and Paris combined! This trade and wealth fuelled the rise and fall of small empires and dynasties and the brief power vacuums that followed, pulling and tugging on migrating populations. Turkic speaking peoples to the north, for instance, coming initially out of modern north-western China, began expanding outwards and in addition to establishing themselves firmly in Turkey (and thereby giving it a name), also travelled and filled Central Asia. And in doing so, they went on to plant the seeds of what would eventually become the ethnic groups of Kazakhs, Kyrgyz, Uzbeks, and Tajiks. But while this was going on in Central Asia, many thousands of kilometres to the South West, in a vastly different world was born a man whose legacy was to have a devastating and far-reaching effect on the region.

## Conversion via the sword

570 AD Born in the small trading settlement of Mecca in 570AD, Muhammad would go on to establish Islam, which by the time he died in 638 AD had become the dominant faith of the Arabian Peninsula. In the years that followed, and over the course of two major subsequent Caliphates*, Islam had spread so far and wide that by the 8th century the Islamic Caliphate had become the largest Empire on Earth. For Europe, this meant that the Iberian Peninsula, namely modern Portugal and Spain, came under the sway of the Arab armies until the conclusion of the Christian *Reconquista* almost 800 years later. For Central Asia, following a decisive battle won by the invading Arab armies on the border of modern Kazakhstan and Kyrgyzstan in 751 AD, it meant that for the next five centuries, the region came under the control of various Arab rulers, and perhaps more significantly, it became and to this day remained Islamic.

Initially, life under these new conservative rulers became somewhat settled. The new Arab overlords were content to keep to themselves, and their battlefield successes subdued an otherwise chaotic region. Thus, the region saw an explosion in scientific, literary, architectural and philosophical output, to such a degree, Central Asian's understanding in these fields shot well past their peers in Europe's, who in many fields weren't to catch up for another few hundred years. This period

---

* Islamic states.

after the Arabs arrived came to be a high point in Central Asian history, and a period described by American historian S. Frederick Starr as an *Age of Enlightenment*. Innovations in mathematics saw the birth of the decimal point and the establishment of algebra. A treatise written in the 9th cen- 900-1200 AD tury by the Central Asia mathematician Al-Khwarizmi was used as the principle mathematical textbook in European universities until the 16th century. And with the increase in mathematical understanding came developments in architecture, astronomy, and optics. Sanjar's tomb, in what is now Turkmenistan, pioneered the use of the double dome, said to have been the inspiration for the double dome of Florence's Cathedral two centuries later[*]. And in astronomy, polymaths such as Al-Biruni were able to deduce that the Earth was rotating, that a full year around the sun was 365.24 days[**], and the diameter of the Earth to be 12,759 km, overshooting the modern measurement by a mere 16 km. And by building a map of the known world and incorporating a rudimentary version of the longitude and latitude of hundreds of known places, Al-Biruni deduced that a large continent existed in the ocean somewhere between Europe and Asia. At the same time, progress was being made in the understanding of health with advancements in surgical

---

[*]  It has been argued that the inspiration for the dome of St. Isaacs Cathedral in St. Petersburg came from the Florence Cathedral, and that the Americans drew on the St. Isaacs Cathedral for inspiration for their United States Capitol Building, thereby creating a possible linear descendant.

[**]  500 years before the Gregorian calendar was introduced.

instruments, operating techniques, and pharmaceutical treatments. One such pioneer was Abu Sina, known in the West as Avicenna and whose *Book of Healing* became the standard medical text in many European universities up until the 18th century. This open enquiry even extended into philosophy and religion, with the centre of gravity for Islam shifting from the Arabian Peninsula to Central Asia. This was illustrated by the six books that make up the Sunni Hadiths "the backbone of Islamic civilisation", five being written during this period by Central Asian writers.

Along with ideas, Central Asian wealth spread outwards into the wider world, indicated best by the scattering throughout the medieval world of the 97% gold coin minted under the Samanid Dynasty. Not since the Roman Denarius had there been such a global reserve currency, with even Vikings converting their loot into these coins, troves of them being found over 1,000 years later near the Stockholm Atlanta Airport. When historians describe Islam's Golden Age, it is largely this period in Central Asia they are referring to.

The domination of this era by Central Asia however began to grind to a halt as divisions in Islam, particularly those between Shiite and Sunni, spread into politics, bringing in its wake a rise in violence. Open enquiry and the peaceful co-existence between city-states was replaced with dogma and fighting, all leading to a destruction of prosperity and a power vacuum that pulled in new hostile invaders. By the 1200s, while there were still small examples of pioneering scholarly work, the new order had brought the Age of Enlightenment to a violent end. And it was during this weakened state when the region had devolved into smaller violently opposed pseudo-empires, that something strange occurred.

*   *   *   *

Sitting 60 km from the capital of Kyrgyzstan are the remnants of the city of Balasagun, the once capital of the Kara-Khanid Empire, a short-lived empire formed just as Central Asia began fracturing. In 1210, Balasagun was suddenly and without warning overwhelmed when a nomadic force which swept in across the Tian Shan mountains and took the city. That they were unknown was almost as strange as the fact that as quickly as they arrived, they suddenly decamped back to where they'd come from. But it wasn't long before they returned, to devastating effect.

### Hordes from the East

While Central Asia had diverted its attention inwards, to its northeast the traditionally disparate groups of nomadic tribes roaming across Mongolia and parts of Kazakhstan had become unified under the leadership of a man named Temujin. And on unifying these tribes, he was awarded a title meaning Universal Ruler, Genghis Khan*. Like those 1200–1350s AD

---

* More accurately, *Genghis* meant 'ocean' signifying the universe, while *Khan* meant emperor.

who came before him, and many who would come after, Genghis Khan saw himself as the legitimate ruler of the world. That he was able, almost without difficulty, to overwhelm every enemy he faced fed back into this myth, fuelling his growing empire's confidence. His army's success lay in a combination of immense numbers and an extreme level of sadistic and outright violence. From the great ocean-sized Mongolian and Kazakh grasslands, Genghis Khan was able to raise vast numbers of cavalry, each of whom had been brought up riding a horse almost since birth. From a young age, Mongolian children were taught to hunt from a horse, and it is said that by adulthood they were able to fire up to six arrows a minute, forwards and backwards, while at a full gallop! His armies of over 100,000 would travel with up to four horses per soldier, allowing the riders to jump from one horse to the next as they tired. A final horse served as a sort of food on hoofs, horse meat forming a major part of their diet, a legacy remaining across parts of Central Asia today. At a time when it took someone in Europe five weeks to travel from Venice to Paris, the Mongolians were able to travel up to 160 km a day. An army of 60,000 to 70,000 Mongol cavalry would suddenly appear as if from nowhere, manned by highly skilled soldiers bearing state-of-the-art military hardware. This technology and skill, however, contributed only partly to their success with a complete lack of mercy and extreme levels of cruelty contributing to the rest. "Man's greatest good fortune is to chase and defeat his enemy, seize all his possessions, leave his married women weeping and wailing, ride his gelding, use the bodies of his women as night-shirts and supports, gazing upon and kissing their rosy breasts, sucking their lips which are as sweet as the berries of the breasts", Genghis Khan is said to have cheerfully said to his Generals prior to a battle. And so, with sheer skill, violence, and overwhelming numbers, like a medieval blitzkrieg, Genghis Khan and his Golden Horde* swept destructively across the Asian continent and into Eastern Europe.

For Europeans this meant an unleashing of carnage across Eastern Christian Europe. Cities such as Kiev, Moscow and Krakow** all fell and were razed by the Mongols. Covered in animals' skins, inflicting overwhelming levels of rape and sadistic violence, and emerging from the unexplored Eastern forests, it was as if the gates to hell themselves had been opened. Pope Innocent the 4th, alarmed at the rapidly falling columns of Christian armies, sent an envoy to the Mongols pleading in the name of God that they cease…

---

\* Golden Horde has become the common term used to describe Genghis Khan and his army that swept across Asia and into Europe in the 13th century. The understanding of the origins of the term is inconsistent, some suggesting that 'golden' referred to the colour of the Mongol tents and 'horde' coming from a Mongol word meaning central place.

\*\* To this day, if you travel to Krakow, stand in the city's central plaza and listen to the trumpet call played on the hour from St. Mary's Basilica, you will note that the call ends abruptly after the fourth chime. It is said that this commemorates the trumpeter who sounded the alarm to the Mongol attack before being cut off as an arrow struck him in the throat.

*"…we are driven to express in strong terms our amazement that you, as we have heard, have invaded many countries belonging both to Christians and to others and are laying them waste in a horrible desolation, and with a fury still unabated you do not cease from stretching out your destroying hand to more distant lands, but, breaking the bond of natural ties, sparing neither sex nor age, you rage against all indiscriminately with the sword of chastisement.*

*We, therefore… beg and earnestly beseech all of you that for the future you desist entirely from assaults of this kind and especially from the persecution of Christians…"*

The Mongols received this in a rather perplexed fashion. It was the Mongol's God-given right to conquer the land, surely their success so far proved this. And so, their response was rather typical—submit or be conquered.

*"Through the power of God, all empires from the rising of the sun to its setting have been given to us and we own them. How could anyone achieve anything except by God's order? Now, however, you must say with a sincere heart: "We shall be obedient, we, too, make our strength available. You personally, at the head of the Kings, you shall come, one and all, to pay homage to me and to serve me. Then we shall take note of your submission. If, however, you do not accept God's order and act against our command, we shall know that you are our enemies".*

As it happened, domestic politics forced the Mongols to return home, almost certainly saving Christian Europe from a complete Mongol invasion. Though just as the Mongol forces were retreating, they did provide one parting gift. In a final attack on the city of Feodosia*, a city established by Genoan merchants as an outer trading post, the Mongols lobbed dead bodies over the city walls. These bodies, riddled with the bacterium *Yersinia pestis*, would cause a victim's lymph node to balloon into hard nut-like swellings called 'buboes' thus lending its name to the disease that it spawned, the Bubonic Plague—otherwise known as the Black Death. Following the withdrawal of the Mongols, the city soon recovered. Unfortunately, when a vessel that had docked at Feodosia headed back across the Mediterranean, it carried the Bubonic Plague into the heart of Europe, killing up to 60% of Europe's population.

*    *    *    *

While 'lucky' would not be the correct term, Europe was at least spared the devastation that Genghis Khan and his Golden Horde wrought on Central Asia. For while many European cities were attacked causing the death of up to a million civilians, they eventually recovered and the kingdoms that they were in remained intact. In Central Asia on the other hand, it was thought that up to a million people died

---

* This city exists today and sits on the East coast of the Crimean Peninsula, ~~Ukraine~~ Russia

in the attack on one city alone, and the various empires that ruled across the region *all* collapsed in the face of Genghis and his Horde.

Major Central Asian cities such as Merv, Samarkand, Balkh, and Bukhara were overrun, swept up in a whirlwind of savagery, mass rape and violence. On his assault on Bukhara, 30,000 refugees were said to have fled into the desert who were then chased and cut down. And following the murder of the populations, Genghis would turn on their infrastructure, destroying their libraries, bookshops, observatories, endowed institutions and schools, followed by the destruction of dams that had feed them, finishing everything off in one mass flood. The famous Arab historian Ibn Battuta, visiting Bukhara in modern Uzbekistan a century after Genghis had swept through, commented that he found the city full of ruins, its markets and madrassas still not rebuilt. No one was able to resist the Mongols, and their campaign was so brutally effective that at their peak they controlled an area that covered 24 million square kilometres, creating the second-largest empire in human history (after the British).

Somewhat counterintuitively, this replacement of warring Central Asian states with a single Mongol hegemony led to what some historians refer to as the *Pax Mongolica* or Mongol Peace. Trade along the Silk Road, for instance, saw a revival, and it is perhaps no coincidence that it was during this period that Marco Polo travelled from Venice and across the Mongolian world in relative safety. Moreover, unlike the

Arab armies who had swept up from the South five centuries earlier, or indeed the Christian Europeans to their West, the Mongols were largely tolerant of almost all forms of religion. Kublai Khan, the grandson and successor to Genghis Khan, was for instance, both a follower of Confucianism *and* Buddhism, and well versed in Islam *and* Christianity, especially the latter which to his mother had converted. And it was under this new openness that many religions began to thrive. Yet this was a hard-won peace, described by the travelling 13th century Persian historian Ata-Malik Juvayni as "a peace of smoking ruins".

Sadly, of all the regions that fell under Mongol control, it was Central Asia which bore much of the brutality while being left with few of the benefits. The now reenergised Silk Road rerouted itself north, for instance, largely avoiding Central Asia and its ruined cities. And while many other areas hit by the Mongols were able to begin rebuilding, the craftsman, artists and architects of Central Asia were rounded up and sent to China, acting as a massive brain drain. Thus for the next hundred years Central Asia fell into destitution, its cities devastated, its talent stolen.

Yet, after all the destruction, the waste and the millions dead, the Mongol Empire collapsed, succumbing to the infighting between heirs of Genghis. But as if the world hadn't had enough of this mass barbarity, a new person rose, this time a man of Central Asian birth, who was to rise and become possibly even more disgustingly violent than the Mongols.

*From violence is born violence…*

Described by A. A. Gill as "a man who made Stalin look Swiss", Tamerlane* was arguably the most destructive tyrant in history. Born in the south eastern corner of modern Uzbekistan amidst the turmoil of the dying Mongol Empire, he was the product of their recent invasion with his Turkic mother and Mongolian father**. He went on to build an empire centred around Bukhara and Samarkand, the latter becoming his capital. Through an extraordinary propensity for *extreme* levels of violence on a colossal scale, eclipsing even that of Genghis and his Golden Horde, Tamerlane came to rule an empire extending from India to Turkey, across almost all of Persia and up into the modern-day Caucasus's.

1350s – 1450s AD

"The Sultan is the shadow of Allah on Earth", read the inscription on his Palace's towers, because like those before him, he saw himself as standing amongst the Heavens. The military campaigns he oversaw from his mid-20s up until his demise at 68, resulted in the deaths of 17 million people, representing 5% of the world's then total population. If on approaching a city it resisted his exorbitant demands, he would destroy it completely, razing everything to the ground, often planting vegetation within the ruins, and poisoning the

---

\* 'Tamerlane' was the name given to him in the West, a bastardisation of his name 'Timur' along with what people would refer to him 'the Lame' owing to a youthful injury leading to two of his limbs being lame.

\*\* A reconstruction created through the analysis of his skull shows a very Mongolian looking character.

surrounding landscape so that it would be gone forever. The canal systems that fed the waters of the Tien Shan mountain range across much of Central Asia irrigating vast tracts of otherwise desert land, and feeding cities with enormous populations, would be systemically destroyed. The most attractive women were thrown into his harem, the remainder raped and murdered. Young men were sent to Samarkand as slaves while everyone else were beheaded. Those yet to meet their fate would often be forced to gather the heads and stack them into pyramids, sometimes many stories high, before they too joined their brethren, with this practise becoming Tamerlane's calling card. After destroying the Persian city of Isfahan in 1387, he ordered every man, woman and child not yet dead be brought to the front of what was once their city. All children under seven years were placed apart in a grid, at which point he ordered his huge numbers of cavalry to ride over them, trampling them violently to death. For the others, many of whom had just witnessed their children being crushed to death, were then beheaded with a historian at the time recording 28 pyramids of 1,500 heads each. In 1400, he destroyed Damascus which through the sheer volume of sexual violence, was referred to ever after as the Rape of Damascus. Ninety thousand were murdered in Baghdad with each of his soldiers being ordered to bring back two heads each for that city's pyramid. He captured 100,000 Hindus on his way to Delhi. But after arriving, he considered them a potential threat to his back lines so had them murdered before burning Delhi to the ground. Pushing his way up into

Turkey, he took on the Ottoman Empire—an empire then the scourge of Europe—and against which a victory by even a coalition of the best armies of Europe had looked impossible. In 1402 Tamerlane arrived with an army of 140,000 and in a single day destroyed the Ottomans, fracturing the Empire and setting off a civil war lasting for 11 years. This scorched earth policy left its mark across a huge portion of the world, but most of all in the area that he had descended from and to this day, parts of once prosperous Uzbekistan, wallow in arid lands, stricken with poverty, all from the actions of a man 700 years earlier.

The *one* positive thing that Tamerlane did for the region, however, was build, "…it is fair to conclude that this last world conqueror was more interested in things than ideas"*, wrote his most recent biographer. While the things he built were not necessarily useful, they were big and beautiful. Many of the monuments I was to see, for which Central Asia is most renowned are buildings constructed by the architects, artisans, and craftsman that Tamerlane had captured and marched back to Samarkand. He demanded his buildings be more spectacular and built on scales never seen before, and at speeds that were frankly impossible. Often on returning from campaigns, he would find the buildings he had ordered not yet finished and would publicly hang the architects in charge, replacing them with a new lot. Consequently, in this rush to finish some of the largest buildings ever built,

---

\*    Tamerlane book. (To look up)

corners were cut leading many to collapse a century, and in some cases, only decades later. And after this disgusting destruction and laying waste to everything that the Mongols just before had missed, he died in 1405 and left an empire which collapsed *almost* immediately. So much of the world was laid to waste by two empires, that themselves left little in the way of progress. To be sure, his grandson Ulugh Beg was a spark of goodness against so much bad and for a while brought back an intellectualism to the region. As a noted astronomer, he went on to build what was regarded as the finest observatories in the Islamic world. His reign, however, was short-lived after his son beheaded him in 1449.

\*    \*    \*    \*

This collapse of what came to be known as the Timurid Empire heralded the end for Central Asian prominence. The Uzbek tribes roaming to the north around the Aral Sea, consolidated under a single leader and began filling the vacuum left by the collapsing Timurid Empire. Tamerlane's descendants put up a fight but were knocked back one by one. Notably, Babur, one of Tamerlane's descendants, held out against the Uzbeks, capturing then losing Samarkand three times before finally throwing in the towel and shifting his army east. And after defeating the Indian armies in the Punjab region, he went on to establish the Mughal Empire, perhaps the most famous to rule over India, and responsible for the building of the Taj Mahal, the Red Fort and the Lahore Fort. With Babur now gone, the Uzbeks were able to reign supreme and went on to establish three different 'Khanates' that ruled over the region for the next few hundred years.

The glory days were over, and while the cities of Bukhara, Khiva and Samarkand benefited from the consolidation of power around them, the region fell into centuries of fighting.

*The world grows up...*

While Central Asia had descended from its heights at the turn of the millennium to a wasteland ravaged by appalling violence, Europe had emerged from its 'Dark Ages' hibernation and was in the midst of its Renaissance and Age of Discovery. This had many consequences for Central Asia, the most immediate the drop in Silk Road trade, a result of the new sea routes opened by European sailors. More importantly however was that after so many years of Central Asia's armies lapping at the edges of Europe, Europeans started turning up en-masse to the edges of Central Asia.

Russians had for a long time been appearing in small numbers along the edges of Central Asia, with Cossacks roaming through the forests of Siberia to Central Asia's north occasionally encountering Kazakh nomads to the South. Indeed, the terms Cossack and Kazakh both share their origin with the Turkic word 'Kozak', meaning "adventurer and warrior", implying a common heritage. But ultimately, these were largely confined to insignificant incursions, rather than formal interactions between the respective leaderships. As the Age of Discovery kicked off the European scramble across the world, Russia, now being ruled by the Romanovs, began pushing their empire south.

This initially meant expanding around the top of the Caspian Sea and into modern Kazakhstan. Central Asia with its ravaged cities, perpetual war and a landscape occupied by roaming nomads much of whose trade compromised slaves, was not an enticing region. Though the Russians were keenly aware that just beyond Central Asia lay the seemingly unlimited wealth of the Indian sub-continent. To get there would require subjugating what lay between them and India, and so at the turn of the 18th century, Peter the Great ordered Russia's first military expedition into the region.

*The Europeans arrives...*

The Tsar's instruction to Prince Alexander Bekovich- 1717 AD Cherkassky was to march into Central Asia, convert the Khanate of Khiva to a subject of Russia, followed by that of the Khanate of Bukhara before sending navigators south to establish a trade route with India. With these easy-on-paper orders, the Prince set off in 1717 accompanied by 4,000 Russian infantry and the latest in European warfare technology.

On being alerted of the approaching invaders, the Khan immediately sent out his cavalry, all duly cut down by Russian grapeshot. Taken aback by the immediate loss, the Khanate sued for peace with a preliminary treaty being quickly signed. Satisfied at the easy win, Bekovich accepted the Khanate's invitation into the city and his suggestion that the Russian army be split into units and camped on the outside. This though was a trap, and after setting themselves up for the night, the Khivans pounced, slaughtering almost the entire Russian force. For a long time after this event *"lost like Bekovich"* became a Russian expression to describe someone who had encountered a terrible misfortune, and for a century this became the last major Russian incursion. To Central Asia's south, however, a different set of Europeans were arriving, that of—amongst others—the British.

*     *     *     *

British merchants had been visiting the Indian sub-continent since the early 17th century, seeking trade along the newly discovered sea route around the horn of Africa. The enormous profits of these enterprises led to increasing numbers arriving at Indian shores, who soon established the East India Company thereby formalising the relationship. After receiving a crown-sanctioned monopoly over Indian trade, the East India Company began establishing trading posts on the ground. This led to massive wealth for the British company, as it exploited the increasing demand for Indian products back home. Yet as it grew, so did the amount it had to lose, and it determined that a private de-
18th Century AD  fence force would be necessary to protect its interests. Soon this defence force numbered in the thousands and more-over was battling local Indian rulers, who despite having overwhelming numbers were able to be put down by the Company's force's superior weaponry. From being involved solely in trade, it now controlled vast amounts of land on

the Indian Sub-continent, along with a substantial private army, being used to put down resisting Indian states. This caused alarm back in Britain, which in response passed the East India Company Act 1773, effectively commandeering the company to the British Crown, and in turn establishing British rule in parts of India. This did not sit well with France or Russia who saw this as a dangerous jump in their rival's position and went about conspiring to thwart it. In 1791, Tsarina Catherine the Great considered plans to "deliver" India from growing British influence, and in 1798 Napoleon sent an invasion fleet with the purpose of capturing Egypt as a steppingstone towards possessing British India. A fleet that was destroyed at the Battle of the Nile by Admiral Nelson.

At the advent of the 19th century, Tsar Paul I proposed to France a joint Franco-Russian invasion of India. Although this didn't eventuate, Britain became apprehensive about its Indian colony and shifting its military focus, soon had a standing army in the region of 260,000 men, twice the size of its army back home. Which in turn only increased the paranoia of Russia which now had a formidable modern army controlled by a competing power stationed just south of the soft underbelly of its Empire. And it was within these global machinations that a new political front opened between the rival Empires of Russia and Britain, that was to bring Central Asia again back to the fore. Something the Russians came to call 'The Tournament of Shadows', and the British 'The Great Game'.

*   *   *   *

Central Asia was now a pitiable backwater, ruled by petty despots inflicting savagery on an illiterate and suffering people with all the power and glory that had been built on the back of so many dead, long since gone. To the Europeans, the area was a large unknown, politically contained by its own now inward disposition and the surrounding buffer states of China and Persia, they only beginning to be understood. Few Europeans had dared venture into the region, and its geography could only be speculated upon. Yet an understanding of this was vital to both the British and the Russians who equally saw that whoever mastered the geography, mastered the routes from which their rival would pour forth and attack. Plans were drawn up on either side and spies, cartographers and diplomats sent forth into this great unknown to discover what they could. Many of these people became well-known names back in their respective countries, thanks to the adventurous tales they recounted in often bestselling books.

While both sides saw fighting, much like the Cold War a century later, it was always by proxy. Britain viewed Afghanistan as its buffer against Russian encroachment and spent a significant amount of wealth and manpower trying to cajole that country into its political sphere. But in what became known as the First Anglo-Afghan War, this first attempt ended in 1848 in disaster, with the retreat of 4,500 British soldiers and the 12,000 British civilians who had accompanied them, all being murdered. Except for one assistant surgeon who with a portion of his scalp missing, stumbled into the Jalalabad garrison six days later*. Russia shared in defeats also with an ill-timed attempt to take Khiva in 1839 seeing the death of almost ~20,000 horses and camels and a good portion of the force, without even reaching the city. And its attempt to take the Turkmen fort of Goek-Tepe near the modern-day capital of Turkmenistan in the latter part of the 19th century saw it forced to withdraw with great losses.

Ultimately though, the British and Russian Empires solidified and expanded their positions in the region. After these initial defeats, having learnt from their mistakes, the Russians overthrew each Khanate, eventually incorporating all Central Asia into her Empire. And Britain—after putting down the 'Indian Rebellion' of 1857, in the process ending the Mughal Empire established by Tamerlane's great-grandson three centuries earlier—took control of India completely and established what came to be known as the British Raj. This period of manoeuvring between these two Empires formally ended in 1895 when British and Russian diplomats met on Lake Zorkul in modern Tajikistan, and established what would be the official border of Afghanistan, India and Central Asia which had come to be known as Turkestan. What had started as panic by either side over the 2,000-mile

---

* This was immortalised by the painting 'Remnants of an Army' painted by Elizabeth Butler.

buffer between them being filled by the other, ended with the establishment of borders separating the two Empires by a mere ten miles. With the British threat to the south now reduced, the Russian Empire began extending (a Russian) culture into their new Central Asia territories.

*Central Asia joins the modern world...*

Telegraph poles and railways were built, connecting towns that for millennia had been linked only by foot and camel. For the first time, the ancient cities of Bukhara, Tashkent and Samarkand and more recent Russian established cities such as Ashgabat were directly in touch with the modern world. And with these conduits of telegraph and rail came Russian settlers who set up hotels and public houses, who brought their unveiled women and drinking habits, and out farmed the original occupants as they tended to their newly granted farmland with superior European tools. The Khanates had for the previous few centuries enjoyed uncontested rule that worked through hierarchy and patronage. Yet once the Russians arrived, they were forced to compromise and were allowed to stay in power—under the 'guidance' of the Russian Empire—but only in exchange for the prime pieces of land which were handed over to Russian settlers. This upending of centuries old life and tradition saw resentment across all Central Asia, which twice spilled over into outright rebellion. `Being outnumbered and outgunned, these rebellions failed but became a mere backdrop for what was about to occur. For as the 19th century rolled into the

20th and brought with it the First World War, the stresses that had been rippling through the Empire exploded.

The first eruption took place in Moscow at the start of 1917 AD 1917, which saw the violent toppling of the Romanov Family who had ruled Russia for the previous 300 years. Months later came the second when the Bolsheviks headed by Vladimir Lenin overthrew the provisional government and installed their vision of a communist paradise.

For Central Asia this meant the arrival of the fleeing White Russian Army, the remnants of those Romanovs loyalists who were fleeing the Bolsheviks, and who despite being backed by the British were eventually destroyed. The advent of communism meant a complete and sudden upending of the Central Asian way of life. Away went the Emirs and Khans and in their place, peoples' commissions, modern schools with boys *and* girls replacing the Mullahs and their madrassas, women unveiled and put to work, new cities built, railways constructed, telegraph poles linked, donkeys replaced with tractors and wildland planted with cotton. Within a decade, entire Central Asia had become communist. Borders were laid down, and the region split along ethnic lines as newly formed 'independent' socialist republics. The Turkmenistan Soviet Socialist Republic came first in 1924, followed by the Uzbekistan Soviet Socialist Republic in 1925, the Tajikistan Soviet Socialist Republic in 1929, and finally the Kazakhstan Soviet Socialist Republic and Kirghiz Soviet Socialist Republics in 1936. Within a generation life in Central Asia had moved from medieval to modern, which as Monica Whitlock put it:

> *Geography changed — Central Asia swivelled from being the north-east of the Muslim world and its bridgehead to Russia to being the southern rim on a new map. Aspirations changed — the mulla to the last khan of Khiva retrained as a kolkhoz manager. Even the way one named and recorded the world was different. The year 1348 became the year 1929 on the Georgia calendar. The rouble came and, later, the kilo and kilometre.* *

This rush into the modern world greatly improved life for Central Asians. Literacy that at the start of the 20<sup>th</sup> century was less than 1% was now racing upwards to rates comparable with Russia, child mortality was dropping, life expectancy increasing, and superstition replaced with science. But these improvements came at tremendous cost as the Soviets began their five-year plans aimed at the rapid industrialisation and agricultural collectivisation.

1930s AD    Property was confiscated to be redistributed, millions of people were moved onto collectivised farms, while millions of others were designated industrial workers and shifted into newly built factories. Unsurprisingly, there was resistance, this violently put down by systematic terror and oppression, which consequently saw the rise of the gulag prison system.

---

* *Land Beyond the River*, Monica Whitlock

Besides the horrendous misery, it also gave rise to mass inefficiency as plans developed thousands of kilometres away were implemented on inappropriate landscapes and societies. Waves of famine swept across the union, that in 1930 hit Kazakhstan especially hard and in what has become known as the Kazakh Catastrophe, caused the deaths of an estimated 2.3 million Kazakhs, representing 40% of its population. While Kazakhstan's famine ended by 1933, a new Soviet policy known as the Great Purge had begun, which saw the imprisonment and murder of thousands of the region's intelligentsia. Though if all this wasn't enough, as the 1930s came to an end, the second Great War began.

*    *    *    *

Initially, the Soviet Union and Central Asia were spared from the war. Ten days prior to the formal declaration of hostilities by the allies against Germany, the USSR and Germany signed a Treaty of Non-Aggression. Yet on 22 June 1941 Nazi Germany broke the treaty, declared war on the Soviet Union and launched Operation Barbarossa, invading the Soviet Union with the largest invasion force in human history, that would within six months' see the death of almost 5 million Soviet soldiers.

For Central Asia, this meant an immediate mass mobilisation of its people. Kazakhs, Uzbeks, Kyrgyz, Tajiks, and Turkmen were rounded up and sent straight to the front line. Poorly equipped and even more poorly trained, the death tolls for these populations were horrendous. When

Germany launched its assault on the Soviet Union, the collective population of Central Asia stood at 17 million, having been reduced from roughly 20 million by the devastating Soviet induced famines. And of these 17 million people, 1.55 million died in the battles and war-induced famines, a full 9% of the total population. Compare this with the United Kingdom, which through the full 1939-1945 period of war, 'only' lost 1% of its population or the United States which lost 0.3%. Given the complete irrelevancy a war in Europe must have been to a nomadic Kazakh or Turkmen, this was all the more tragic.

Though while the second great war ended, within only a few years an iron curtain had divided Europe and a new colder but more persistent war arose. Unlike other wars, this was not just about control but about ideology where defeat was existential. As laid out years earlier by Mikhail Frunze, a high ranking Soviet born into Bishkek, capital of Kyrgyzstan: "Between our proletarian state and the rest of the bourgeois world there can only be one condition – that of long, persistent, desperate war to the death".

1950s AD    Perhaps counter-intuitively though, for Central Asia, the Cold War brought about a lot that was good. During WW2, Stalin had moved much of the union's industry away from the European front, and deep into less vulnerable Central Asia. This meant an immediate heavy industrialisation of the region. With that came the desire to extract more of the regions' mineral resources, in turn leading to greater industry. Huge swathes of land were irrigated, rivers dammed, and nuclear power plants built. And for the same reason industry was shifted here, major military sites with Air Bases, missile ranges and missile test sites were built, increasing the area's strategic value (albeit not always to Central Asia's favour). It is no coincidence that most of the targets of the United States U2 plane shot down in 1960 had been in Kazakhstan.

As this was a war about ideology and convincing the still undecided world where they should be leaning, Central Asia was advanced as an example of how the third world could develop. Elites from developing nations were invited to Central Asia by the Soviets, keen to show the success of their model. This attentiveness of the Soviet Union towards Central Asia saw a huge rise in prosperity, with the 1960s and 70s being a sort of developmental golden age. As noted in *Land Beyond the River,* a farmer summed up half a century thus, "There were dreadful wars and then a huge repression, then came the big war. And then things were alright".

Yet while Central Asian scholars were being pushed to write positively about the Sovietisation, and economists and politicians from third world countries were being toured through Central Asia, something strange happened. Something that wasn't foreseen by the journalists, by the politicians, by the think tanks or the academics. The Soviet Union imploded.

*Central Asia goes it alone...*

The imagery associated with the fall of the USSR often 1990s AD includes the Velvet Revolution of Czechoslovakia, the execution of Romania's dictator, and the fall of the Berlin Wall.

Reflecting it as a very European affair. For Central Asia, which had been enjoying unprecedented growth for the past three decades under governments whose budgets were subsidised by the Soviets, in some cases up to 70%, the Soviet Union's collapse was a catastrophe. Economically, the region fell into a major depression with the GDPs declining by 30%-45% over the 90s, and inflation running into three and sometimes four-digit numbers. In turn, this turmoil led to the rise of Islamic fundamentalism pulling in jihadists from across the border in Afghanistan, many having been radicalised by their long war against the Soviets. An Islamic movement in Uzbekistan suddenly appeared with the explicit goal of overthrowing the government and installing a caliphate in its place. The Uzbek government reacted violently leading to a decade long oppression of its people. Meanwhile, in Tajikistan, the country spawned its own Islamic movements, plunging it into the worst outbreak of violence in all the ex-Soviet states. Conflict between the countries also arose, as the stabilising influence of the Soviet system and free transit between states which had smoothed out ethnic differences, disappeared overnight. An Uzbek living in Kyrgyzstan or a Tajik in Uzbekistan were now arguably out of place, which caused ethnic riots to flare up along with the mass migration of people back to 'their' respective countries. Russians also left in droves, reducing their numbers in Central Asia from 10 million in 1989 to almost half of that a decade later.

Such a tumultuous period was hardly conducive to liberal reforms. Unlike their counterparts in Eastern Europe,

Central Asia did not have a history of democratic institutions and had been ruled by despots for literally the entirety of history. Consequently, the apparatchiks in power in 1989 simply continued ruling over their countries. The notable exception was Kyrgyzstan which against the odds, stumbled towards a democracy with its first (partly) free election in 1995.

*The new order begins…*

If the 90s was chaotic for Central Asia with its repression, violence, terrorism and ethnic rioting, by the early 2000s, life began to improve. The global commodity boom saw billions pour into resource-rich Kazakhstan, Uzbekistan and Turkmenistan. That same boom saw a demand for labour in Russia which attracted Central Asians who remitted back billions, accounting as one point for 33% of the Kyrgyz and 49% of the Tajik GDP. And along with economic success came the slow creep of liberalisation. Despite presidential corruption and distorted elections, the Kyrgyz resisted in what came to be known as the Tulip Revolution and removed an increasingly despotic President. Uzbekistan since the death of its first dictator saw the steady opening up of its markets to outside investment and held its first democratic election. Even in Kazakhstan, the man who had ruled since the country was born, decided to voluntarily step down, at least nominally, from power. Sadly though, this liberalisation has yet to reach Tajikistan and Turkmenistan, both still ruled by oppressive governments.

And in the backdrop of this sits China, whose Belt and Road project aims to fasten China to the world using trains, highways and energy pipelines, all of which must cross Central Asia to reach Europe. It is no coincidence that this initiative was announced by President Xi Jinpeng from a podium in Kazakhstan. The fourth-longest road in the world now extends from China, across Kazakhstan, and into Western Europe. What would take a truck 30-50 days to travel from China to Europe, now takes eleven. The Silk Road which once connected these two hemispheres has re-emerged from the dead and as Central Asia benefited from the original Silk Road, it will again be a major beneficiary of the new one.

Yet despite all this, the truth—as pointed out by A.A. Gill—is often different from the "facts". Amongst the almost three thousand years of facts about violence, facts about invasion, about reinvigoration and destruction, facts about creativity and dogmatism, and migration and genocide, what would be the truth to Central Asia? I decided to ask the locals myself.

# KAZAKHSTAN

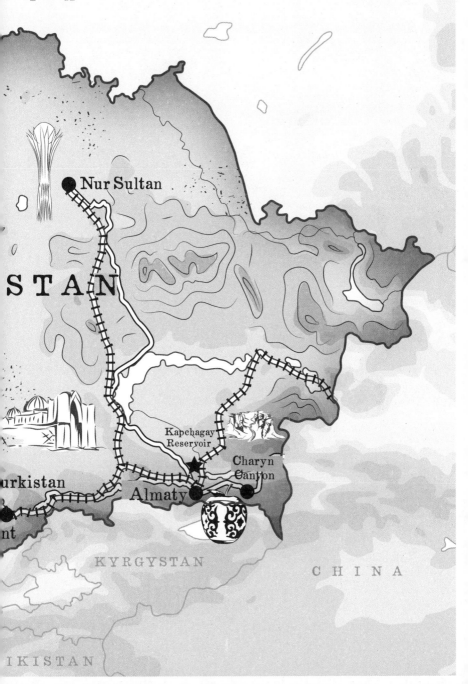

# ALMATY

"Another gin and tonic Sir?", asked the pretty Air Astana stewardess. "Yes, thank you", I said for the fourth time which being partly Australian was entirely acceptable, but being on a Kazakhstani flight where the drinks were free poured with a heavy hand, was getting me rather drunk. I was five hours into a seven-hour flight from Seoul to Almaty flying Air Astana, the Kazakhstani national carrier. Having read the Lonely Planet's description of flying in the region as 'least interesting' which is fine, and 'least safe' which is not, I was expecting that on a scale of 1 being the American's airlines to 10 for those of the Middle Eastern, Air Astana would've been sitting somewhere between United and Delta. What I wasn't expecting was a modern plane with attractive stewardesses serving excellent food while pouring stiff drinks, and an airline that had won the Skytrax World Airline award for Central Asia and India for the past seven years running. One of the many misconceptions that I was to correct over the subsequent months (though not always in my favour).

*    *    *    *

Eleven kilometres below me lay Xinjiang which, had several events played out slightly differently during that period of the Great Game in the 18th and 19th centuries, may have fallen under the control of the Russian Empire rather than that of the Chinese Qing. And had it done so, it would have almost certainly become another Soviet Republic and would probably be known today as The Republic of Uyghurstan. Sadly, for the modern Uyghur, this has meant that they have remained under the control of the Han Chinese which has led them to their very recent situation of being routinely confined to institutionalised detention. Contemporary reports in 2018 reveal a million or so Uyghurs currently undergoing 're-education', another of those shamelessly Orwellian terms that the Chinese Communist Party so love. Thankfully for me however this meant that to complete my journey through the 'stans did not require me to camel my way through the Taklamakan Desert whose name was Uyghur and meant 'Go in—and you won't come out.'

Two hours and the equivalent of eight gin and tonics later (Australian/Acceptable) I landed into Almaty, Kazakhstan's largest and most cosmopolitan city. It was a late Friday afternoon and excitedly I rushed through customs, grabbed my bags and walked out into the arrivals hall where I was customarily fleeced. It was hardly my fault—I was drunk of course—but also because a very nice but quite intimidatingly large bloke who looked like Wladimir Klitschko but spoke like Mike Tyson led me through the hall and into his mate's 'taxi'. 'Taxi' generally refers to a driver who has passed some form of a test, driving a government-regulated car, charging you a government-regulated rate. My 'taxi' was a musty two-decade-old Mercedes with a chain-smoking, gold chain-wearing Kazakh in the front seat who charged me whatever the app on his phone said which may have been a calculator and have simply said 'A LOT'.

Already being in the car that was now moving at pace down a highway with a driver that didn't speak English and a bloke the size of a young bull elephant in the passenger seat, didn't put me in a particularly strong position to start discussing terms. But despite that and to my slight surprise, I managed to arrive at my hotel in a reasonably efficient manner and happily paid the driver the requested 15,000 Kazakhstani Tengi. Had I landed and been more well... sober, I would've worked out the currency conversion and perhaps known that this was five times the local rate and that a 2,000 Tengi tip was probably unnecessary. While one does feel a tinge of bitterness whenever something like this happens, it helps to remember that the 'extra' amount I paid was the equivalent of only 1/32 of the average Australian weekly wage, was being paid in a country where it was equal to 1/3 of the weekly wage and to a bloke with 20/32 of his teeth.

*   *   *   *

Almaty, with 2.4 million people, was the country's capital until the President declared in 1997 that the site of a former Soviet gulag sitting in a frozen semi-arid, empty expanse of nothing was in fact superior. Being a former USSR city, Almaty contains those standard trappings of Soviet planning—featureless monolithic buildings which prize function over form, homogeneous grey cityscapes—and no doubt to the pleasure of former Australian Prime Minister Tony Abbot—a large coal power station gracing the city skyline. But it is also rather sweet. Streets heavily lined with trees that sprinkle their leaves across the pavement and roads. Deep ditches adjacent to the pavements running with crisp mountain water, and in that Soviet-style—a multitude of heavy stout statues celebrating poets, philosophers and Mongol warriors. And all with an extraordinarily impressive mountain range looming large over the city. This the Tien Shen range (meaning Heavenly Mountains in Mandarin), runs along the border of Kazakhstan, Kyrgyzstan and China and boasts an array of peaks that reach upwards of 7.5 km into the sky, offering an extremely impressive backdrop from almost any position in Almaty. China successfully applied for UNESCO World Heritage for its side of this range acknowledging that these mountains are home to some of the world's last remaining wild apple forests. Genetic testing has traced the apple's origins to this range, thus implying all apples can trace their ancestry back to the apples growing in the mountains above Almaty. The Silk Road passed through this city, and it was this route which is believed to have helped scatter the apples grown here throughout the European world and then even further on the backs of European colonists across the Atlantic and into North America. This the residents, or at least the government, avidly promotes with the apple appearing on almost every billboard, in statues throughout the city and indeed even in the city's name which in Kazakh translates to 'Father of Apples'.

\* \* \* \*

While staring out the window towards the mountains looming over us, the giant in the front seat said to me knowingly, "If lost, always walk towards those mountains". I thought this a bit silly as it depended on where I was lost from, though in hindsight it was a piece of wisdom had I imparted on my friend, would've helped him on his attempted journey home later that night.

\* \* \* \*

For two years, my friend Andrew and I had discussed travelling together through Central Asia. We had both independently travelled to unusual places for years, initially setting out from Australia on rather typical journeys, following those Australian migratory routes through South-East Asia. But we were soon venturing out further, with each new trip corresponding to a decreasing thickness in our travel guides and a heightened anxiety in our parents. Andrew would be solo hiking in Persia, while I'd be on a camel with my burka-wearing girlfriend in the Wadi Rum desert. I'd have twelve constipated days hiking in the Papua New Guinean jungle, while Andrew would be getting accosted by a newly liberated, toothless homosexual in the revolutionary streets of Tunis. Our first trip together was in 2014 where along with 20 others we entered North Korea. And at the last minute we were invited to compete in the Pyongyang Marathon where we both placed third (I in the 10 km, Andrew in the half marathon) and stood on a podium surrounded by 88,000 mechanically clapping North Koreans. Unusual places attracted us, they offered something raw without the tourism industry's gloss. They presented different ways of perceiving the world and ideas of how to structure themselves, and it was because of this they were interesting and therefore appealing. And here was Central Asia, an entire region, made up of political systems in flux, by people who had been forgotten, and histories on epic proportions unknown in the West. So finally, after deciding on this trip at the start of 2018, nine months later we both landed from our respective cities into Almaty. And only hours after that, were sitting at a bar drinking the local beer and smoking what the uninitiated may refer to as an 'excessive' number of cigarettes.

*   *   *   *

We had a rough plan but arriving at the start of what was the culmination of almost a year's research, we were simply excited to be here. That said there was one symbolic thing we were definitely going to do that night, and that was to eat Beshbarmark—the national dish of horse.

I had told many people I would be touring the region on an equine diet, and the response was almost universally one of repulsion. I'm not sure if this was properly thought through, as a grass-fed horse in an open field seemed more appetising to me than a pig wallowing in mud, or worse imprisoned in a factory pen. As it does to Gordon Ramsey too, who for over a decade has argued for horse meat becoming a part of the British diet. And frankly, it tasted a lot better than the dog soup I'd eaten in North Korea and most meals I'd had in America.

Asking the bar tender where we could find the best Beshbarmark, we were sent to *Zhety Kazyna*, billed as the 'The National Restaurant', in a building that displayed an interesting variety of foreign influences from Arabic style coves to a Californian interior, and decorated in those somewhat gaudy Kazakh colours of baby blue and golden yellow. "Beshbarmark, Manti and your finest Kazakh wine please". Manti being a Korean style dumpling found throughout Central Asia and a product of the large numbers of Koreans in the region. They'd been here since the 1930s when Stalin—fearful that they'd fall under the influence of neighbouring Japan—had 300,000 Koreans forcefully transferred from the Far East. Fitzroy Maclean, the great British war hero, had snuck into Central Asia in 1937 while stationed as a British diplomat in Moscow, and—while standing at a train station in Almaty—witnessed firsthand this forced movement of people. "All grinned incessantly and I gathered from the few words I could exchange … that they were pleased to be going to Central Asia of which they had evidently been given enthusiastic accounts". Those enthusiastic accounts turned out to be slightly incorrect, and sadly, of the hundreds of thousands of Koreans sent to these parts, upwards of 40,000 were believed to have died. Simply a drop in the ocean of misery the Soviet Union inflicted on Central Asia during the reign of Stalin, a man who in my view at least should be regarded equal to Hitler in terms of modern-day tyrants. Though as a consequence, you find that a conspicuous portion of the Kazakh and Uzbek populations have Korean ancestry adding a very Eastern Asian appearance to the faces of the people, and an influence on the food. Unfortunately, Koreans aren't known for their winemaking so while the horse and the dumplings were excellent, the wine was not. That… or my only partly English-speaking waiter had misinterpreted what I'd said as 'your most disgusting wine please'.

Finishing the bottle of vinegary red wine, we headed out into the brisk evening hailing down the first car we saw, off to see a girl named Sayora, a local Kazakhstani who I'd met two weeks earlier on Tinder. Tinder, of course, being one of modern life's conveniences, up there with penicillin and the combustible engine, and was as well regarded in this part of the supposedly conservative world as it was in the supposedly hedonistic west.

\*　\*　\*　\*

Described by almost every blog as "the best nightlife in Central Asia", once the sun sets on Almaty, the city's conservative image disappears about as quickly as a horse at a Kazakh BBQ. Coming from Australia, and in particular Sydney, being able to smoke in the street without being brought down by two police German Shepards, battened in the head and tasered for good measure, the Almaty nightlife felt especially free. The bars and clubs are stylish and well designed, the prices extremely affordable and without the overbearing regulations of the West, there is a pervading sense of freedom. And to really top it off, the women are beautiful. I hold the theory that when a nation is aggressively warlike and the soldiers prone to snatching and bringing home the best-looking women, the local women will turn out to look as if they were handpicked (which in a sense they were). The Vikings and the Swedes are a fine example, the Mongols and the Kazakhs another. And assuming, based on objective evidence that we were the only foreigners in the city, we felt particularly excited to be a part of it all.

The first place we accompanied Sayora to was to a collection of rooftop bars. Allowed to the front of the line, greeted with big smiles and pats on the back, we were led up a flight of stairs and into a huge open rooftop area with themed bars lining the perimeter. Spending no more than USD$10 we bought a round of drinks and sat down at a table where promptly we were earnestly and deferentially approached by a group of young men who with hands on their hearts, began greeting us in broken English. One of the more confident lads sat down with me and in broken English tried to determine where I was from. Our conversation was sadly limited to the English he knew, and the Russian that I didn't but he pushed on regardless, animatedly explaining to me something that I couldn't understand. With the help of Sayora, it turned out he was explaining to me the despair that he felt in having to inherit his family's horse farm, preventing him from working in finance. Which I thought was an amazing and rather rapid development in our friendship.

Andrew rose to buy more drinks and disappeared into the night. I tried calling but his phone was off and despite his generally white and red appearance which should have been acting like a lighthouse amongst the sea of black hair, I couldn't see him. As it transpired, his phone had been stolen and he had found himself lost. Thinking that we'd left him, he left the bar and knowing no Kazakh, no Russian, and having no phone, had simply decided to walk in the direction of the hotel. Almaty is arranged as a grid, so he had four options, chose one and got it wrong. He walked for an hour in a growing panic as all cars continued to ignore him and his outstretched thumb, presumably seeing him for some crazy drunk foreigner (which he was). I like to think about this moment as if silently looking down from the height of a plane, seeing my friend wandering alone in a city surrounded by mountains and desert, growing ever more anxious and knowing too well that the only person he knew on the continent—but for me—was 4,000 km away in Hong Kong. With the sun now peering over the mountains, Andrew was eventually picked up and taken home. He should've walked toward the mountains.

*   *   *   *

We woke up late that morning and headed out for breakfast. The Green Market was our initial target, a sprawling food market that had existed in one form or another for almost 150 years, though had taken its current Soviet utilitarian look in the 1970s. Like many of the Central Asia cities I was to visit, the streets and parks were lined with bulky solid statues of national heroes. And almost immediately on exiting our hotel, we were confronted by a large statue of a stereotypically Mongol looking character astride a horse, his arm outstretched appealing to an imaginary crowd. This character was Amangeldy Imanov, an early 20th century Kazakh 'Robin Hood' figure who had been robbing rich Russian landowners on behalf of Kazakh peasants, a decade before the Bolsheviks spread through the region and made that official policy. These raids had been a consequence of the increasing resentment felt by the local population to the forced transfer of their grazing lands to Russian settlers. Something that was compounded as Russia stumbled into WW1 and began requesting from Central Asia, donations of meat, hide and horses for the Imperial cavalry, with the word donation being a polite synonym of the word demand. Between 1914 and 1915, for instance, 260,000 heads of livestock had been 'donated' to the Russian army, and all without remuneration. Until this point, a policy exempting Central Asian men from military service on the grounds that they were Muslim had kept a lid on open discontent. But as the war began taking a heavy toll on the Russian Empire, Tsar Nicholas II in 1916 abruptly adopted a draft of conscription on Central Asian men which for the local populations became the final straw.

Initially, this resulted in small outbreaks across modern-day Uzbekistan and Tajikistan of sporadic violence against Russian garrisons and settlers. News of these rebellions and early successes spread across the region and back into Kazakhstan where resistance to Russian rule had begun, reinforcing its momentum. Organised armed groups totalling up to 30,000 Kazakhs began forming, with 20,000 alone falling under the leadership of Imanov. In what came to be seen as the greatest success of this uprising, Imanov successfully led an armed group of 15,000 Kazakhs in an assault and capture of the small town of Turgai in the centre of the Kazakh plains. Alarmed at this sudden rebellion, the Russian Empire diverted a heavily armed force of 30,000 Russian soldiers from the Eastern Front to Central Asia. Outnumbered and outgunned, what came to be known as 'The Central Asian Uprising' was finally put down. Ultimately it achieved little other than killing 3,000 Russian settlers and soldiers, at the heavy cost of tens of thousands Central Asians dead (some reporting upwards of 270,000). Within a year however this all became moot, as the Bolsheviks violently swept away the Tsar and the system he represented, and then— with equal violence—across Central Asia. Suddenly what had been regarded as a native uprising against Russian rulers, instead became broadcast as a peasant uprising against the bourgeoise. Imanov, who had been a dangerous rebel now became a Bolshevik hero, and whose death was not at the hands of an opposing Kazakh tribe, but that of 'counter-revolutionaries'. In Soviet history, he came to be viewed as a man who helped overthrow the bourgeoise enemy and sweep the Soviets to power, a hero whose face the Soviet's glorified on a 1961 USSR postage stamp. Today, however, he is more accurately known as a hero of Kazakhstani nationalism, an idea that the current government is more than happy to promote.

*   *   *   *

The streets had steadily become busier the closer we got to the market, which by the time we arrived were now filled with traffic, the pavements with people. Hawkers and their food stalls lined the streets outside the Green Market, all stood shouting, vying for attention.

We pushed our way through the crowds, up the steps and into the market building, now adding smell to our other already overwhelmed senses as we entered into the two-storey high closed roofed market. Rows upon rows of meats hung, lay and piled upon each other, as Kazakh butchers jostled for our attention, shouting from between hanging carcasses. This was more or less a supermarket, though without the packaging or possibly the hygiene. Walking past sheep heads, and horse tongues, we reached the vegetable section and grabbed a small bag of kimchi and later a couple of apples, choosing from the multiple two-person high apple pyramids that filled the fruit corner. Despite being hungry, we weren't prepared to test our weakened stomachs with unknown meats handled by an unknown number of hands, so having seen, smelt and tasted the market, we left.

We headed to Paniflov Park, a leafy city park whose various names throughout history and its grand Cathedral sitting at its centre, was a fitting reflection of Kazakhstan's changing political history. It had originally been built in the 1870s named *Old Cemetery Park* and served as a cemetery for those early pioneering Russian settlers. In 1899 its name was changed to Pushkin Park, in commemoration of the 100th anniversary of the birth of the revered Russian poet, Alexander Pushkin, and a further sign of Russian entrenchment in the region. In 1913 an exhibition was held there in celebration of the 300th year anniversary of the Romanov dynasty, the ruling family of the Russian Empire, which only four years later would be violently expunged. And as part of this changing of the guard, as the Russian Empire was replaced with that of the Bolsheviks, the park was once again renamed, this time to "Park of Fallen Heroes" in memory of the soldiers of the Red Army who had died during the Bolshevik revolution. Once the Bolsheviks got down to business however and began reshaping the world around them, and in that soul-sapping communist method—renaming everything in the way which a command economy requires—the park changed its name once again to the uninspiring *Public Park of 1 May* in recognition of International Workers Day. But in 1942 the name became its current

*Paniflov Park,* which like its predecessors, walks on uncertain ground.

This name came from a group of 28 soldiers who in 1941 played an oversized role in their defence of Soviet Russia during the Battle of Moscow, a colossal struggle that is regarded by many as one of the defining moments of the Second World War. The 28 soldiers, most of whom were Kazakh and Kyrgyz, were able to hold off a German tank attack, maintain their strategic position and destroy 28 German tanks in the process. It was said that one of the political officers in the group had shouted to his comrades, "Russia is a great land, but there is nowhere to retreat— Moscow is behind us!" before hurling himself under an oncoming tank with an armful of grenades. This impassioned defence was recalled by one of the wounded members of the 28 who gave an interview from his bed in a military hospital before dying of his wounds and in the process helped turn this event into a Soviet Empire-wide legend. Poems were written about these heroes, streets across the Soviet Union were renamed to "Paniflov's Heroes" and the Moscow city anthem was rewritten to include the line, "We will remember grinding of tanks and glint of bayonets, we will remember your twenty-eight brave sons". The problem, however, was that it was largely a fabrication, a revelation that only came to light when a 1948 report into 'the 28' was declassified in 2015. The report detailed that some of the 28, all of whom had been posthumously awarded the title of "Hero", were actually still alive, one of whom had in fact been arrested in 1947 for "betrayal of the motherland", another who hadn't even fought in the war. And further, the German tank division's mission that day rather than being stopped, had actually been successfully completed. "… it did not occur. It was a pure fantasy", wrote the military judge overseeing the probe to Stalin himself. Having survived for 73 years and having firmly become a part of the national mythology, across the ex-Soviet world this legend was not going to die an easy death. "…even if this story was invented from start to finish, if there had been no Panfilov, if there had been nothing, this is a sacred legend that shouldn't be interfered with. People that do that are filthy scum", Russia's cultural minister had said in response to the revelations, shortly before firing Russia's chief state archivist who brought these documents to light. Looking up at this powerful statue with its strong block like human figures launching forward in attack, their faces full of resolve, I could understand the reticence people had when faced with the truth. It was such an important aspect of the identity of Soviet and Central Asian mythology, it would be as if New Zealanders discovered that Edmund Hillary had faked his ascent of Everest, or Australians uncovering Phar Lap had been born elsewhere. Though this was no longer the Soviet Union where the 'truth' was whatever served the politics at the time, since the collapse of the Soviet Union, these ex-Soviet states have begun to more honestly re-examine their history. While it is yet to be seen how the Paniflov 28 will eventually be regarded by Kazakhstan, they have begun reconsidering a period in its history that for so long had been hidden away, that of the 1931-1933 Soviet induced famine.

\*    \*    \*    \*

Often referred to as the 'Forgotten Famine', the starvation that spread through the Soviet Union during the first years of the 1930s struck Kazakhstan especially hard. With contemporary geopolitics playing out in Ukraine, the spotlight has been cast back on the country's suffering in the early 20th century. Anne Applebaum's excellent book *Red Famine* details extensively the horror of Ukraine's famine which saw the deaths of between 2.5 and 3.5 million people. But like the Ukraine's, the Kazakhstan famine was inflicted upon the country by the Soviet's forced collectivisations, and while responsible for 'only' killing 1.5 million Kazakhs (though possibly up to 2.3million), this represented 40% of the Kazakh population. The famines had come about as a direct consequence of Stalin's five-year plan whereby he forced mass industrialisation and collectivisation upon the peasantry across the Soviet Union. Because the Kazakhs were still practising pastoral nomadism, carrying out seasonal migrations along routes defined by centuries of history, being forced to relinquish all their possessions and pushed onto collectivised farms saw them hit especially hard. At the same time, the mass inefficiencies that naturally came about from trying to impose plans written in Moscow onto local conditions across the plains of Kazakhstan, brought about the mass death of animal herds with up to ninety percent of the animal population perishing over five years. Being forced into a foreign way of life, while at the same time undergoing a mass indoctrination where the 'Kulaks', said to represent the oppressive capitalist class, but in reality, anyone who owned more than the absolute bare minimum, meant that attempting to survive through this famine became all the more difficult. Kazakh society was completely destroyed, with traditional family links broken apart. Numerous stories of corpses lining the roads, feeding roving packs of wolves fill the historical literature—yet more shocking still were the reports of gangs of cannibals roaming across the region, preying on the vulnerable. While there is evidence supporting the theory that famine had been knowingly and purposefully imposed on Ukraine to suppress the otherwise resisting population, it is less clear in the case of Kazakhstan. In saying that, Stalin had been made aware almost immediately of the outbreak of famine across Kazakhstan in 1931 but did little to alleviate the suffering until 1933. Ultimately, it led to the destruction of a way of life, upwards of 2.3 million Kazakhs dead, the remainder now a minority in their traditional homeland and a changed demographic across the region. Today, significant numbers of Kazakhs reside in neighbouring countries such as China, Uzbekistan and Russia, as a result of the migrations they were forced to take.

Yet until recently, little academic attention had been paid to it. I did find a memorial to the famine in Almaty—a statue depicting a gaunt woman holding a child in her arms, its rib cage pushing through the skin, but this had only been built a year earlier, in 2017. Cynically, it has been said that the advantageous position Kazakhstan holds with Russia is probably one of the reasons why no official reports into the famine have yet been conducted. A Putin spokesman recently called talk of the famine in Ukraine as genocide and an attempt "to rewrite history". This though is changing. With research into the Ukrainian famine receiving increasing attention, especially following the Russian invasion of Crimea, more attention is being paid to what occurred in Kazakhstan. One more historical crime committed under the Soviet system that was finally seeing the light of day.

It was late afternoon by now, and something in our stomachs—almost certainly the kimchi—was telling us we needed to get back. And so, with a clench of the cheeks we quickly but delicately minced our way home.

\*    \*    \*    \*

Given the previous night's self-flagellation, and because the following morning would be driving a rental car four hours into the desert, we determined that our last night (for two days) in Almaty should be low key and sensible. The bartender in the hotel lobby recommended a Georgian restaurant nearby, which we duly made our way to after finishing the Negroni's that we had sensibly just ordered. Not being au fait with Georgian cuisine, and with the restaurant staff only able to speak Russian and Kazakh, we indicated we would have whatever the chef recommended, which turned out to be the produce of a small farm accompanied by that of a small vineyard. Given it was our last night in Almaty, we thought we could follow dinner with at least one drink, so jumped into a taxi to an upmarket outfit which wouldn't be out of place in any major Western city.

It was humming with people when we arrived, and in a moment that made me feel both chuffed and shameful all at once, the bartenders called us out by our names. What really took us back, however, were the two foreigners sitting at the bar, one an impressively large American man, and a rather diminutive woman who turned out to be from the US Embassy. "What are you up to here?" I asked the bloke, who said he was here as a special guest of Almacon. It being the equivalent of Comic Con held in other cities around the world, bringing the authors of fantasy and comic books and movies together with their fans. And the special guest I was talking to turned out to be Jesse J. Holland, the author of *Who is Black Panther*, a book written on behalf of Marvel about the movie the *Black Panther*, a worldwide box office success and 9th highest-grossing movie of all time. My star struckness notwithstanding, I could sense irritation from the American Embassy woman who I had a sneaking suspicion saw Jesse J. Holland as her *black panther*, and so we said goodbye and took our drinks to the veranda.

In a jovial mood, we struck up a conversation with two Kazakh blokes who turned out to be Almaty lawyers. They had both lived abroad, but with the political and economic landscape changing, they explained, finding a well-paying career in Kazakhstan was becoming easier. Moreover, they had wanted Kazakh wives, and had returned to find them with Chingiz recently having a kid, which despite his friend's teasing, he insisted had changed him for the better. Followed almost instantly by the suggestion that we head to a nude bar. This wasn't especially appealing to either Andrew or me, but Chingiz was extremely insistent, so having arms made of rubber that had been sitting in the sun all day, we left.

Completely unsurprisingly, the place we arrived at was depressing and seedy. This 'nude club' appeared to be a large community hall, with two leather couches awkwardly positioned in front of an ad-hoc stage, and speakers on stands blearing out loud Central Asian electronic music. For an hour we sat there as two girls worked the empty room and uncomfortably clambered over us and our new friends, until thankfully it was decided that we should probably leave. We opened the door back out into the now, and to our horror, sun lit the street. Yet rather than sensibly hailing a taxi, and sensibly heading in a straight line to our hotel bedrooms for a sensible few hours of sleep, we instead decided to take the advice of our friends and head for breakfast.

It was almost 6 am by this time, and we walked into an American style diner that was filled with people still out from the night before. As it happened, this was the way Kazakhs drank. You started at midnight and ended with breakfast before going to bed and later waking to kickstart your new day with lunch. Usually, there wasn't a world heavyweight fight featuring the pound for pound best current fighter who happened to be Kazahki though in this instance there was, with Gennady Golovkin aka 'Triple G' defending his WBC and WBA middleweight titles against the Mexican super-star Saul Alvarez. Which the stats of each fighter we were now learning from a bunch of young Kazakh lads who we had snowballed with during breakfast, and who were now sitting with us in a dimly lit room, in a non-descript build-ing staring at a flat-screen tv. All sensibly further from our hotel. The fight was now underway, and despite the steady stream of alcohol, we decided that given we were meant to be driving in a few hours, it would probably be sensible to make it back to the hotel for some remnants of sleep and in the most sensible move of the night, we left. As it happened Golovkin lost, his first defeat in 40 pro fights with the fight running the full 12 rounds, ending roughly an hour after we'd left, and roughly eight hours after we should've….

# IN NEED OF A MAP

We gotta go", my bloodshot eyed friend said to me as I stood in my underwear holding the door more to keep myself upright than keep it open. After two nights of excessive drinking, smoking and eating of horse, it was now midday, I was in my underwear, we were an hour past check-out and the car we had arranged was sitting in front of the hotel. In happier times we had planned to drive to Kara Dala, a 4.7/5 Google Rated hot spring in the desert that borders China and that for its rating was suspiciously inexpensive.

Thankfully I didn't have to drive and was able to sit in the passenger seat and belt feed cigarettes to my face while Andrew, on an hour's sleep, negotiated the Almaty traffic that involved fewer wheels and more hooves the further out of the city we moved. The trip we were on was to take us four hours into an extremely dry corner of Kazakhstan bordering

Kyrgyzstan to the South and China to the East but of course, with the lack of sleep, GPS or this thing called a 'map', it took almost double. And so, for seven hours, we hurtled down an empty highway through a desert landscape that was flat, vast and featureless. To our south were the Pamir Mountain ranges that steadily swept up off the land and relentlessly continued to climb until they were touching almost 8 km into the sky, just shy of their Himalayan neighbours. And to the north the endless expanse of hazy desert punctuated by nothing except herds of those wild horses that eight hundred years earlier had made Genghis Khan so violently successful.

\*     \*     \*     \*

Seven hours of desert driving, with weak, sleep-deprived conversation and the almost battery-drained phone not able to offer us even a podcast, we arrived at our destination. Kara Dala, the 4.7/5 Google rated hot spring that we accessed via a dirt track, whose perimeter was made of corrugated iron topped by razor wire, and which was currently being circled by a vicious looking dog with the head of a wolf, the body of a wolf and which turned out to be a wolf.

"Christ, look at the size of that thing", I awkwardly said to the thuggish looking guard in military fatigues with a baton at his waist, and who was standing behind the locked gate not looking like he was going to let us in. He grunted back at me, and in scrunching his face up revealed a complete set of gold teeth which I thought nicely suited his Bond villain persona. After a few barks into his walkie talkie, he begrudgingly opened the medieval gate and escorted our car into the compound which had obviously recently been cleaned, as there wasn't evidence other than the circumstantial, of heads stuck on stakes.

"What the fuck is this place", I cheerfully said to Andrew, as we walked to the office to check in and past an absurd collection of plastic animals including a leopard, some wolves, a couple of deer, pink flamingos and the entire cast of Shrek. Stepping over a plastic turtle and into the office we were greeted by two enormously round babushkas who forever broke the spell at least in my mind that very fat old ladies equalled friendly grandmas.

The reason my friend and I were staying at Kara Dala—where strips of wax were hanging from the ceilings and successfully catching flies—was that we were using this lovely place as a launching pad to Charyon Canyon, Kazakhstan's supposed answer to the Grand Canyon. Being no more than three times longer than the Grand Canyon was wide (albeit at its widest point), it wasn't exactly challenging that canyon's perch on its pedestal, but still, it represented an 80 km long crevice in the earth, and an interesting landscape to explore.

\*    \*    \*    \*

We rose early, in an attempt to avoid the babushkas and suspected guard wolves, but were hampered by the chain-locked gate, forcing us to summon the security guard who glared at us in our idling car while the gate screeched open.

He was however soon receding in the mirror, coughing on the dust kicked up by our car (or so I hoped) as we took off down the desert road.

The sun was low over the easterly mountain range, casting its light across the vast dusty plain and creating a haze on the horizon that our straight and seemingly endless road disappeared into. Though as if from an apparition, a small town appeared, it's streets lined with surprisingly lush trees as if this were an oasis in a desert (which perhaps it was). The town was buzzing with people, weaving in between the food stalls lining the roads, selling piles of fruits, vegetables and cigarettes. We soon joined them in search of breakfast, garnering open gaped stares that made us feel as if we were thousands of kilometres from home in the middle of nowhere. To my delight, I found a store selling cans of spam that would nicely accompany my sandwich, causing Andrew to scoff that I'd eat such a thing, striking me as a little rich given the tins of canned horse lining his backpack. Driving to the outskirts of the town, we stopped at a half-built monument that sat opposite a billboard of the Kazakh President, helpfully reminding the people of his generosity. Under the President's glaring face, we scoffed down the food and a couple of cigarettes, throwing the leftovers to the wild dogs that had concerningly appeared near the car, before carrying on to Charyon Canyon.

An hour later we reached the entrance to the Canyon. It was devoid of people but for a German couple who were backpacking through the region, had just slept overnight in the canyon and were now walking to Almaty 210 km to the West. The sun was now high overhead in a cloudless sky and despite it being autumn, the temperature was sitting in the late 20s. Andrew and I parked our car and made our way down a dusty trail to the start of the track. Rusty red cliffs lined either side of our path, the product of years of erosion at their base. They grew taller as we carried on walking down the steady decline that eventually landed us at a bend in the Charyon River, the turbulent alpine river that was responsible for carving the 80 km of deep canyon through the Kazakh desert plain. It would eventually merge with the Lle River before draining into the Kapshagay Reservoir, a large Soviet-built reservoir that like many major Soviet projects, had caused significant environmental damage to a region was only just starting to recover. To my surprise, along with ourselves were several other people, drinking lemon sparkling water under the shade of umbrellas, being served by a waiter. Not only that, but behind them sat well-made yurt huts on raised wooden porches as well as bungalows with their own private terraces, overlooking the river and surrounded by a manicured grass lawn. On enquiry, it turned out to be an Eco Lodge in which you could rent a bungalow for the night for slightly less than I'd paid the taxi driver the day I arrived in Almaty. And while I didn't want to jump to any conclusions just yet, I had a sneaking suspicion that there wouldn't be wax strips catching flies hanging from the bungalow's ceilings. We wandered around, sat down and had a drink, then turned and started on our way back. I remarked to Andrew that the surrounding landscape reminded me of Petra, presumably formed through similar forces, to which he told me the extraordinary fact that Petra had been built by the Jordanian government as part of a tourism drive in the 1950s. That there had always been a small ancient settlement there, but the towering rock-carved buildings that made the site so famous were all modern buildings, designed to attract unwitting tourists. Of course, my mate was talking garbage, though convincing garbage, and he had left me in deep consternation about it until I reached internet hours later. With that circling around in my mind, we made it back to the car and started our arduous march home.

*   *   *   *

We somehow managed to avoid the more direct route home and instead rerouted ourselves through a couple of small towns, one of which we decided to stop in for a meal. The town itself was somewhat sweet, with a main road lined with tall poplar trees dissecting it. Behind the trees sat crudely made stores, and immediately in front of them, Kazakh women tending to open-pit fires cooking and selling meat. None of the questionably sourced meat being handled by sweaty grease-covered ladies looked appetising even for our post-hike stomachs, so we instead opted for a makeshift restaurant. Ordering randomly from a menu in Cyrillic, the waitress went outside to one of the Kazakh women and piled a plate with the meat from her fire before returning it to our table. A group of large older Kazakh men entered too and sat down at a table near ours. They were a lively bunch and were received by the restaurant with a round of beers. And after settling into the drinks, one man—the physically largest of the group—started a low deep song, sad and melancholy, with other men joining him in unison once he'd sung the first verse. The song ended, more beers were poured, food was brought and they got down to eating.

We paid the ludicrously cheap bill and wandered back to our car, walking past a memorial to those who had died in WW2 and presumably those that had died who were local to the area. It was interesting to see not because it was different, but because it was familiar, so like the monuments that appear in small towns throughout Australia and New Zealand. Though there was one striking difference, that of the red Soviet Star sitting at the crown of the plinth. An interesting thought, that this plinth stood here reflecting on those that had died for an ideology that no longer existed, that moreover was largely regarded as morally bankrupt. Though of course perhaps some future scholar may consider the same when viewing those monuments in small town Australia and New Zealand, which claimed that these dead, died fighting for Queen and God both *almost* anachronisms today. What was especially sad about this monument though, and the Kazakh role in WW2 broadly was how severely affected they were. One point two million Kazakhs were drafted into WW2 of which 310,000 were killed, all from a population at the time of six million. Compare that with say New Zealand which saw 12,000 deaths from a population at the time of two million, and with New Zealanders fighting at least for a British Empire that they shared a kinship with, rather than an Empire who for the past three decades had been imposing increasingly dreadful hardships on them.

\*    \*    \*    \*

After a final two hours of hurtling through the desert, we eventually made it back to Almaty and then finally to our hotel, arriving in a state much like our car, tired, dusty and spluttering out the rear. But after checking in, showering and undertaking our ablutions, we headed out for a stroll into the somewhat balmy evening.

The air was warm and calm, and a deep low bass could be felt coming from a concert in the distance that was lighting up the sky above it. The streets seemed busier than usual, and as we turned a corner onto a main road, we came across a police cordon that was preventing vehicle traffic from entering. We melted into the pedestrians that were weaving their way through the cordon onto the empty road and became part of a swarm of Kazakh youths that were converging on a concert. The concert was being held by the Kazakhstani boy band, *Ninety One*, a group that like many groups in the West had been formed after a televised national talent quest, and then pulled together under an entertainment label. Their name was in recognition of the year Kazakhstan gained independence from the Soviet Union, and their music genre was known as Q-Pop, a take on the Korean style K-Pop which their music was modelled, but also with a Western and more significantly, Kazakh influence. Together, the boys of *Ninety One* represented somewhat of a spearhead of the new confidence felt by the next generation of Kazakhs. Don't get me wrong, this wasn't David Hasselhoff singing *Looking for Freedom* in the summer of 1989 and thereby single headedly bringing down the Berlin War and ending the Cold War. This was a band of 19-year old boys singing about falling in love with a fan base that was largely limited to 19-year-old Kazakh and Korean girls. But as pointed out by the lawyers we'd met days earlier, Kazakhstan was now a land of opportunity, no longer did Kazakhs have to look to Russia or even the West for a source of pride. In a short documentary produced by the BBC titled *Young, Cool and Kazakhstani,* it was said that 87% of the youths polled had said that their future lay within the country. And what Ninety One *did* represent was a break from the stolid, earnest Soviet past. Apparent especially when they went on tours throughout the country, which were almost always accompanied by protests. When for instance they performed in the Kazakh town of Qyzylorda, groups of old men tightly packed themselves together and began theatrically chanting in unison as if on a stage show, protesting them for 'being too gay'. But with 50% of the population in Kazakhstan being under 30, it was the youth who would define the future of this country.

\*   \*   \*   \*

Our flight to the capital Astana the next day was at 12:30 pm meaning we could have breakfast, even squeeze in a session at the gym all with enough time to drop the car back to the car hire and make our way to the airport. Of course, this was on the assumption that we were dropping our car back to a normal, efficient profit-driven enterprise. Had we known that instead, the car rental was operated by a lady to whom the idea of working terrified her, then perhaps we would've skipped the gym. Our first problem was that the car rental operator was frightened of phone calls, so we, therefore, couldn't pinpoint exactly where the car rental office was but for the fact that it existed *somewhere* amongst a block of communist era cookie-cutter buildings. With the clock ticking, we were now literally running between buildings always with the doubt at the back of our minds that a car rental place would be operated out of an apartment building. After the second sweep through the buildings, we discovered an inconspicuous door that led down a dingy hallway and—praise be to Allah—to the office of our car rental. We opened the door into a tiny windowless office deep in the guts of the building and found a single lady seemingly on the verge of a flu induced death. Given that she couldn't speak English and us nothing else, what should've been a quick handing over of the keys turned into an extremely drawn-out hour-long conversation via Google Translate which seemed to involve an increasing number of fees. We frantically agreed to the additional unknown costs and waited as the lady slowly withdrew the credit card machine from under the desk stopping every so often to blow into her handkerchief and accidentally onto us, before slowly handing back the machine. Finally paying and rushing to the taxi driver who was understandably irritated to have been kept waiting, we jumped into his car, rushed to the airport and missed our flight.

*        *        *        *

Almost two months later I returned to Almaty, this time with a different friend who had flown up from Bangkok to spend a week in the country. The city was different now. When it had been somewhat temperate the first time around, this time it was cold, and the mountains were now covered in snow that was always threatening to roll down and blanket the streets. I was eager to find an eagle handler and was told we could find the real deal in the Tien Shan Mountains, so arranging a driver to take us, we headed up towards the Blue Lake. I had visited this lake the first time I was in Almaty. Then the sun was still giving off heat and light which had been reflecting off the flat turquoise alpine lake with its shores packed with groups of young Kazakhs mucking around and couples taking selfies. Now, however, it was deserted, and the blue sky and bright sun had been replaced by a low cloud cover that enveloped the tops of the once green but now snow-covered mountains. Moreover, what was once a simple Central Asia road to get there with say a normal 10% chance of death by motor vehicle accident, was now a treacherous, icy road with the only saviour being the rusty guardrails that were there to protect your car from going over the steep road zig-zagging up the mountainside.

Making our way up in a refreshingly modern car, we passed several cars littered along the roadsides, abandoned by their owners who had decided to continue the trip on foot. At the point where our car slid left towards the cliff edge, instead of right as the driver had intended, we decided that our driver could park, and we could walk.

Gingerly climbing the icy road on foot, we first heard and then saw a pickup truck slowly and then much more quickly careen backwards down the road towards us. We jumped out of the way, to see the truck continue down until it crashed into a car jammed precariously against a guard rail, itself groaning as it took the added weight.

We carried on up, our breath casting clouds of mist as we trudged our way through the snow. "Look at the size of that bloody eagle", my mate exclaimed, pointing at two dark figures coming down from the hill with an eagle perched on one of their arms. The two men were hunters, and we waved them down to better look at their bird. The handler indicated we could hold it and placing a small leather pouch over its eyes, he shifted the eagle from his arm onto mine which was now gloved in leather. The eagle weighed close to 5 kilos and was attached at the foot by a rope which the handler was holding onto, and which when he gave a quick tug caused the eagle to throw out its wings in order to regain its balance, revealing its glorious 2 m wingspan in the process.

Using eagles to hunt with was common in this part of the world. A Philippine backpacker I'd met in Kyrgyzstan had told me about a hunting demonstration. The handler had removed the leather cover from the eagle's eyes, which anticipating what came next suddenly became agitated and excited. Giving his arm a lurch, the eagle launched into the air and took off across the field, while he reached into his bag and released a small rabbit. The rabbit darted out before hopping around in dazed confusion, while the eagle arced back and then came in like a missile slamming its claws and talon into the rabbit, before proceeding to rip it apart alive. This custom had been introduced to the Kyrgyzstan region by the Mongols during their conquest in the 13th century, though it was a custom that was slowly fading with time. Back in Kazakhstan however, hunting with eagles was alive and well and formed part of the national identity. Hunting with falcons (falconry) popular in Arabia and Europe, is viewed by the Kazakhs as child's play compared to hunting with eagles which are several times bigger and stronger. It is said that the eagles the Kazakhs use to hunt with can catch not just a hare or fox, but even a roe deer or wolf. And rather than there being a well-stocked trade in eagles, as there is with falcons, the eagles used by the Kazakhs are caught in the wild by their sayatshy (owner), adding a more personal and perhaps more raw overall experience. And it was in these hills above Almaty in which many of these hunters would hunt.

It seemed though that on this day, these hunters had been unsuccessful. That was until two Australians turned up and they successfully managed, via an 'eagle experience', to catch 250 Tenge off them each.

# ASTANA

Astana, the capital of Kazakhstan since 1997, described by CNN as the 'World's weirdest Capital', and a shining example of what happens when you give bureaucrats the responsibility of designing a city from scratch. Sitting in a flat semi-arid region in the northern part of the country, Astana experiences an annual average day time temperature of 3.5 degrees making it the second coldest capital in the world after Ulaanbaatar. You would think one answer to this would be to tighten the city up like a blanket, but instead, those city planners employed from the top have spread the city thinly out and crisscrossed it with wide four-lane roads. Which despite how lovely this all sounds makes for an extremely depressing city, that really does not have to be seen except of course if you're attracted to awfully wacky architecture (especially those of the 90s variety).

Officially the capital was changed to Astana to shift it away from earthquake-prone Almaty. Unofficially this town, once known as the site of a Soviet gulag, became the capital to shore up Northern Kazakhstan, populated at the time by a large Slavic population which was considered at risk of breaking away. Had there been any criticism of this policy (of course only a theoretical possibility in Kazakhstan), that criticism must surely have disappeared following Russia's annexation of Crimea in "the interests of Russians living there". Once declared the capital, it became President Nazarbayev's pet project in which he set out to build his vision of utopia through the help of several famous architects from Norman Foster to Zaha Hadid.

The problems that I see however were multiple. As a salute to their paymasters, the architects often built in the unfortunate colours of the national flag (cyan and gold), much of the architecture came from the 90s and from the look of it, it seemed as if many of these were handed over to the interns. And finally, a lot of the direction came directly from Nazarbayev himself. "Although he has no formal training, Nazarbayev was directly involved in the design of many of the built works in Astana..." wrote the glowing, sycophantic book *Astana, Architecture, Myth & Destiny*. Written ostensibly independently by Canadian historian, Frank Albo, though given its suspiciously glowing reports of an extremely absurd city, possibly as a commission of the Kazakh government[*].

---

[*]   The book was dedicated "To the munificent people of Kazakhstan, the way-showers of the twenty-first century."

Much like London, many of the buildings have been nick-named by the locals, though slightly less endearingly. The Golden Towers, two round buildings, tapering up and cov-ered in lurid yellow golden windows (which must be appall-ing for its occupants), have been named the Beer Cans. The Baytrek Tower, named after the Kazakh word for the poplar tree, with what looks to be white scaffolding holdings up a yellow golden panelled ball, has been named the lollipop. And the Palace of the Arts, with "its hollowed-out slanted cone meant to symbolise the essence of human creativity and the natural elements… a circular temple to the muses"*, is known as the Dog Bowl. To be entirely fair, a few of the buildings that have been built in more recent times look fine, sophisticatedly futuristic even. But they're devoid of people. Take the Expo site for instance. Built for the World Expo, the same expo that showcased the Crystal Palace in London to the world in 1859 and the Eiffel Tower in 1889, the lat-est expo was won by Kazakhstan in 2012 for the 2017 event and was dedicated to the development and promotion of sus-tainable energy. As explained by the same Frank Albo, "The ambitions of Astana's World Expo echo those of the World of Tomorrow, which was first presented at the New York World's Fair of 1939-40". Almost 45 million people visited the New York expo while original estimates for attendance to the Astana expo were 5 million, which seemed reasonable given its isolation from almost everywhere (little surrounds

---

\* More Frank Albo.

the city for 1,200 km but for a few provincial towns), and the far less importance of such a world fair in today's world. However, these estimates were slowly revised downwards first to 3 million, then to 2 million. In the end, 670,000 tickets were sold though there were doubts on how real those ticket numbers were. Today it stands as an empty convention centre occupied largely by people waiting for other people to arrive.

*     *     *     *

"Amazing!" exclaimed the attendant shaking his head in disbelief as we told him where we were from, while he ushered us through the security screening area that was manned by an excessive number of guards. The site was frankly rather impressive. Designed to imitate the *Cenotaphe to Newton*, a building proposed by an architect in 1784, the Expo Building was the tallest spherical structure in the world, one massive glass sphere held together by an internal lattice structure. Transparent lifts took us to the top of the structure, where we could see through the glass skin and out across the city. With the theme of sustainability, each floor was dedicated to a different form of renewable energy, all connected by glass staircases that sat on the inside of the outer curved building's edge. Andrew and I slowly made our way down, examining the expensive-looking exhibits in silence but for the noise from the speakers of each display. At one point we came across a Chinese couple who were as startled to see us, as we were to see them, otherwise, it was empty but for the apathetic attendants who sat around idly on their phones.

We finished the exhibition and wandered out into the grounds of the site, made up of pristine concrete and manicured gardens, and devoid of people. A bitterly cold wind whipped around the area, which slammed shut the door behind us as we retreated into the nearest restaurant. Inside sat a disinterested waitress dressed in a traditional Kazakh outfit who finished the message on her phone before slowly rising to take us to a table without asking if we wanted one. The restaurant was empty and dead quiet. To save on power, presumably, the overhead lights had been turned off, with the restaurant being illuminated by the big glass windows overlooking the grey grounds on a grey overcast day. The first four things we ordered they didn't have, so we settled for dumplings which arrived suspiciously promptly after requesting them. We looked out across the empty grounds; everything was quiet but for a whistle from the wind catching a gap in a window. And looking back and up at the big semi-transparent dark green sphere from where we'd just been, I couldn't help but feel that we were sitting in some dystopian future.

*    *    *    *

We had arrived in Astana a few days earlier, making our way through the modern though rather bleak city to our hotel. Like the city, the hotel had a nouveau riche feel with its driveway taking us past a large ceramic pot spilling fake gold coins onto the lawn. A Genghis Khan looking man in a top hat took our bags, and led us inside into the large cavernous atrium, the nine floors looking down onto us along with the gold-trimmed couches and the grand piano which at the time of our arrival was being played by a man in white gloves. Very petro-state chic I thought, though being Central Asia, despite what was in front of us was still somewhat affordable.

Having dumped our bags, we avoided the almost convincing Irish Pub built into the hotel and strolled across to the Khan Shatyr Entertainment Centre.

Meaning 'Tent of the Khan' and open since 2010, the centre was one of the two Norman Foster-designed mega structures to form part of the city. At 150 m high, covering an area of over 1.1 m square feet and designed to resemble that of a yurt—the traditional homes of the Kazakhs, it was the largest tent in the world. Having to withstand a temperature range of -40 degrees in winter to +40 in summer, it was designed with state-of-the-art technology allowing it to maintain a micro-tropical climate inside. Which amongst other things allowed you to sit on an artificial beach by an artificial sea, made of sand brought in from the Maldives. We discovered though, somewhat sadly, that like in other oil-rich nations in the world, it was conspicuous consumption that formed the bulk of the 'entertainment'.

A lift took us up to the centre's viewing platform revealing that we were at the city's edge, with the icy dessert steppe starting almost at the ground floor and spreading west to the horizon. On the other side was the city, made up of tall glass and steel buildings some copies of each other, separated by one long boulevard symmetrically cutting the city in two. Along this boulevard stood the Baiterek Tower, and at its end the Presidential Palace, a building modelled on the White House. Though being eight times larger and built by absolute rather than elected power, it was a building channelling less Carter and more Ceauşescu.

We exited out past a lonely I LOVE ASTANA sculpture, and strode up the boulevard, the walls of buildings lining each side helping direct the icy wind sweeping in off the surrounding desert steppes into the faces of Andrew and I. The Baiterek Tower soon loomed above us, its 100m high bird's nest styled structure designed to embody a folklore story about a mythical tree of life and a magic bird of happiness. At its top sat a viewing platform that housed a block of gold adorned with the handprint of the President, which you are encouraged to place your hand in, face the President's Palace and make a small wish. Which with a small stretch of the imagination, you could possibly see occurring elsewhere in the world, perhaps – say – in Florida while looking out towards Mar al Largo.

We carried on, walking through the 'Park of Singing Fountains' which are said to put on a light and fountain show like those in Vegas and Dubai, though sat disappointingly empty the day we walked by. The two golden buildings nicknamed the 'Beer Cans' stood in front of us, with bulky curved buildings sweeping back on either side of them, which together appeared like a city gate and walls. Between the 'cans and the Palace sat a vast concrete platform, entirely empty but for us and the three (those whom we saw) heavily armed policeman eyeing us suspiciously. Having braved the wind and the cold, we were disappointed to find the Palace closed that day and so we were forced to stand there and admire from afar. While it had been designed to create an impression, standing there on the grey concrete on a grey day, looking at the gaudy gold-trimmed, baby blue-domed Palace, while being punched in the face by an icy cold wind and looked down upon by heavily armed angry-looking men, that impression felt rather grim.

Over to the right of the Palace sat an under-construction elevated monorail which being protected by hoardings covered in Chinese characters, and more significantly seeming entirely unneeded above the empty roads, implied a Chinese Belt and Road project. And in front of the monorail sat the Kazakhstan Concert Hall, a baby blue structure referred to by the Italian architects who designed it, as their 'Flower of the Steppe', and by the locals as 'The Cabbage'. From above, the structure of the concert hall formed a 'vesical piscis', the term given to a geometric pattern in which two disks intersect in a particular way. If of course you sit in your parent's basement obsessing over a short-lived 18th century group of Bavarians that weren't cool enough to make it into the Freemasons, then instead this is just one more example of the deep conspiratorial symbolism of Astana, 'The Illuminati Capital of the World'.

\*     \*     \*     \*

Since the buildings of Astana broke ground, internet sleuths have been cleverly identifying the masonic symbolism built into this capital, which may I remind you is the newest capital in the world, hardly a coincidence given the need for a new capital for the imminent New World Order. Take the two yellow golden towers (the 'beer cans'), that look suspiciously like the two altars of a Masonic Temple that flank the throne of the Grand Master. And what are these obvious Masonic altars flanking, the Presential Palace, the Presidential 'throne'. Atop the Palace—a blue dome, said to represent the 'Female Principle', directly facing the Bayterek Tower, the 'Masculine Principle'. And the folklore that I earlier said was the inspiration for the Bayterek Tower. False. It is actually the 'morning star', the symbol for Lucifer, not surprising when you consider the city's name—A S T A N A, or perhaps aka 'SATAN…a'. If this isn't enough, consider the pentagram inside a circle found outside of the city. Which despite the mainstream media insisting was once the Soviet Star sitting inside a children's park, is in fact none other than an indication of the worship of Satan. And if you were still unconvinced, then let me end this with the next building we visited—the Palace of Peace and Reconciliation, a glass Pyramid with—you guessed it—a symbol of the sun aka the symbol of Lucifer, sitting at its centre.

For those of us still brainwashed by the *mainstream media*, the Palace of Peace and Reconciliation is the second Norman Foster-designed building and was built in 2006 to house the 'Congress of Leaders of World and Traditional

Religions'. This three-yearly Congress was initiated by President Nazarbayev and brings together delegates representing Islam, Buddhism, Christianity, Shinto, Judaism, Taoism and Hinduism, with the Congress and the Pyramid dedicated "to the renunciation of bigotry and violence, and to the promotion of peace and human equality". Which is all very well and good, so long as you aren't a 'non-traditional' religious group who have been banned under laws passed in 2011, or those violent and hedonistic Jehovah's Witnesses who have been prevented from practising since 2017. In the 2018 United States Commission on International Religious Freedom, the report placed Kazakhstan on their 'Countries of Concern' watchlist, commenting that "Amid a general crackdown on dissent and nonconformity… the Kazakh government continued to commit serious violations of religious freedom in 2017". Commenting to Foreign Policy magazine, one interfaith expert stated that the Congress was "a complete waste of time, developed along the old lines of the Soviet Religion and Peace events, which were likewise a front for repressive regimes trying to look nice". It turned out to be a waste of time for us too, because unfortunately at the time we arrived—and despite the multiple people staring back at us blankly from behind the glass doors—it was closed. That or they'd spotted Andrew's fashion sense and confused us for Jehovah's Witnesses. It hardly mattered to us though, as the day was growing long, the temperature was dropping, and I needed to head home to change before setting out to meet a friend I'd recently met online.

\*    \*    \*    \*

I caught up with my new Kazakhstani friend Nazgal later that evening at a glitzy bar on the top floor of the recently built Ritz-Carlton Hotel. The bar was teeming with expats in suits, most of whom were Americans, all seemingly to do with the oil industry. The floor to ceiling windows presented an impressive view of Astana with its bizarre buildings well-lit from the ground up. "That's where I live", Nazgal said pointing out her suburb which was named Micro-District 2 and was wedged between Micro-District 1 and Micro-District 5. Another one of those delightful consequences of a command economy.

We left the bar and walked across the road to the Eternal Sky Restaurant sitting on the 25th floor of a newly built building. On exiting the lift, we were—to my surprise—immediately greeted by a man and woman both heavily dressed in thick woollen vividly coloured clothing, better suited to the steppes than a somewhat upmarket restaurant. They took us to our seats against a window, affording us another view over the city, though this time in a different direction which showed the blackness of the desert at night beyond the sparkling light of the immediate buildings. I was happy for Nazgal to take care of the ordering which included a substantial serving of horse. I explained to her that this was a novelty to me as an Australian, "But, do you not eat cow?" she questioned me with a rightfully baffled expression.

Nazgal was working for the national airline which along with many other national companies had based their headquarters in Astana. She had grown up in a town near the Aral Sea in the South of the country but had moved here with her parents when she was young. That Aral had once been the fourth largest lake in the world, had supplied the Soviet Union with 7% of its fish and was once even home to a small Russian Empire naval fleet. That was until the 1960s when the Soviets decided it would be the basis of one of their megaprojects, whereby man and machine would break and shape nature to its will and convert the surrounding desert landscape into a vast modern mechanised agriculture field. Yet after sapping the rivers that fed the sea, it soon became starved of water and began evaporating out of existence. It is today regarded as one of the world's worst ecological disasters and viewed from space, looks more like a collection of stagnant ponds than a single body of water. Across this parched landscape lie boats and wharfs, rusting relics of a once-thriving fishing industry. And if that wasn't enough, at its centre on what once was an island sits the decomposing structure of a deserted Soviet biological weapons testing centre. One that was home to anthrax, smallpox and the bubonic plague, and which would have the occasional leak such as when it leaked a brown haze, infecting a passing Russian scientist with smallpox, who went onto spread the infection on her return home. Or when in 1988, 50,000 antelope grazing nearby suddenly dropped dead in the space of an hour. That though was when it was operating, and the protective barrier of the Aral Sea has long since gone. Having not been properly dismantled, it leaches its toxic contents into the topsoil of the surrounding landscape which is sometimes whipped up by dry winds and deposited across once seaside towns. It was from one of these towns that Nazgal and her parents were evacuated.

*   *   *   *

I woke the following morning and met my friend for breakfast. We decided to pick up from where we left off and began the day at the Palace of Peace and Reconciliation. The Palace sat in the Presidential park, which would be beautiful in summer, but was windswept and cold the day we were there, with the pathways running through it broken and overgrown. Across from us stood the Kazakh Eli Monument, a monument to the Kazakh people made of a solid white marble colonnade curving around one large central plinth with a golden eagle perched at its top. The plinth was 91 m high as a nod to 1991—the year of independence—and at its base were four bronze reliefs representing "Courage", "Creation", "Future" and the fourth, "The First President and the people of Kazakhstan". Of course, there's nothing unusual with celebrating famous national figures through public sculpture, think of the United States and Mt. Rushmore. Though it's perhaps a little different when the figure is still alive, is an unelected dictator and is depicted surrounded by adoring people as if he were the North Korean leader on a field trip.

We carried on through the central marble arch of the colonnade and up to the very recently built Peace Wall, a sophisticated structure that was designed to look like a ribbon folding down on itself. The curved underside was made up of an LED digital screen that was playing a speech President Nazarbayev had given at the United Nations, his voice projecting from hidden speakers. The wall was only a month old and was dedicated to the President's vision of a nuclear-weapon-free world, a policy that unlike other Central Asia government internationally pushed policies wasn't simply cynically self-serving.

It was an idea that Nazarbayev had promoted since the country's post-Soviet inception in 1991, noting at the time that 'Kazakh people have been through hundreds of tragedies similar to that of Hiroshima.' While arguably overstepping the mark, he was referring to the devastation wreaked on the country from Soviet-era nuclear weapons testing. For during the days of the Soviets, it had been determined that Kazakhstan was the ideal location to test nuclear bombs with the first one detonating in 1949, followed by another 450 or so more*. While the testing ended with the collapse of the Soviet Union, the repercussions didn't and along with numerous puncture marks across the landscape**, large swathes of the population were left with high rates of suicide, cancers and deformities. On receiving the keys to the nation in 1991 from the retreating USSR, rather than keeping the fourth

---

* Almost 2000 nuclear bombs were detonated during the Cold War, meaning that a full quarter of detonations occurred in Kazakhstan.

** For those interested, they can be seen here: https://virtualglobetrotting.com/map/semipalatinsk-nuclear-test-site/view/google/

largest nuclear arsenal in the world that his country had just inherited, Nazarbayev instead and almost immediately repatriated the ~1,400 nuclear warheads back to the new nation of Russia. From here he continued his push, overseeing the signing of the Central Asian Nuclear Weapons Free Zone, that banned the testing, development and even transit of nuclear weapons through the region. And more recently establishing the International Atomic Energy Agency's Nuclear Fuel Bank in Kazakhstan, a 'bank' storing nuclear fuel, accessible by treaty nations in the event of their fuel suddenly becoming restricted. The idea behind it being that countries no longer have a need to enrich the fuel themselves, thereby avoiding the temptation of pressing only marginally further into the enrichment of nuclear weapons. "… an investment into a safer world", commented Warren Buffet who personally donated USD$50 million to the project.

Though while actively promoting the abolishment of nuclear weapons, this has not excluded the country from profiting off nuclear power. And with 15% of the world's uranium supply sitting squarely within its borders, it has grown its uranium industry over the past two decades to become the largest supplier of internationally traded uranium in the world. It is this uranium along with some of the largest oil and gas reserves in the world that have allowed Kazakhstan to become the richest state within Central Asia. That the two fastest-growing major economies in the world ever hungry for more energy sit next door has ensured a steady regional demand. And like so many oil-rich states around the world, the easier the money the proportionally greater the need for their leader's expression of piousness. Which in many cases means the building of mosques, the larger the mosque the presumably more righteous the leader. And in front of us now stood the recently built Jazrat Sultan Mosque, the largest mosque in Central Asia.

This mosque had opened in 2012, and unlike some other mega mosques I was to visit in the region, this one in its gold and black trim, with its four ornately decorated marble minarets at each corner, all looked rather sharp. Though with the mosque bearing down on us, the pictures and statues of the ever-present leader, the futuristic and garish buildings scraping the sky in the distance, and the general showiness of this shiny new city, it felt simply like we were in a cold version of Dubai. Impressive sure, but soulless and oppressive too. And a city that we did not intend to miss our flight out of, so rather than inadvertently staying any longer, we jumped in a cab to the airport and left.

# SHYMKENT AND
# TURKESTAN

I s there anything more annoying than being situated near a group of people that will not stop talking. Now let me ramp it up and place you and those people in a confined space, change the language of the people to something you don't understand, and throw in the fact that those people are also energetically drunk. Having drunk the airport bar of all their Jameson's Whiskey, my friend and I were now those people and flying to the somewhat obscure city of Shymkent, it was almost certain that we were the only ones speaking English. An hour and a half later after what we considered to have been a rather delightful flight, we landed into Shymkent, the third-largest city of Kazakhstan, and made our drunken way to the hotel.

"Where can we get a drink at this time in Shymkent?" It was 10 pm on a Sunday night in a conservative Muslim city in a Muslim country, and we didn't like our chances. We could, of course, raid the mini bar, and I believe one of us suggested sneaking cigarettes out the hotel window, but it turned out we didn't need to. "There is one bar in Shymkent that is open 24/7"… our eyes widened… "And it's right there", said the man behind reception as he pointed over our shoulders to the White Horse Bar, the only bar open 24/7 and that was sitting in the lobby of our hotel. Leaving behind our bags and two ghostly apparitions that looked like us, we beelined directly for the bar, ordered two double gin and tonics and engaged everyone in the bar, that being a single lone American. "Well, if you're buying…" he said with a laconic drawl when we asked him over for a drink. He'd been living in Kazakhstan for three years, working at the American Embassy and was clearly over it. "The corruption maaaaan…. It gets you down…". It certainly had got him down as he told us about the inefficiency, the isolation and loneliness he felt. To be fair to Kazakhstan, he was stationed in Astana, and living there for three years would've in my view constituted a cruel and unusual punishment. That this guy had the personality of a spud probably didn't help either. A couple more blokes walked in, then a few ladies after a night out in the city and being the only foreigners in what felt like the country, a snowball of drunkenness slowly built with my friend and I at its centre. Many hours and many drinks later, I was seated next to a rather fat Kazakh man who was telling me that he thought my friend and I should probably go to bed, "Why", I thought I said but probably simply blinked, as my eyes drifted across to my friend who was now standing rather than sitting on his chair. "Yes", I thought, "this fat man is correct, time for bed".

*    *    *    *

We arose the next morning suspiciously each with a hangover. Our drinks from the previous evening had clearly been spiked, possibly with alcohol. The train we were meant to have taken was at 5:15 am that morning but having left the bar at 5:30 am we were now in search of a new mode of transport. The place we were trying to get to was Turkestan, the once capital of the Kazakh Khanate from the 16th to 18th century before the Russians kindly incorporated it into their growing empire, and home to an array of historical sites built by Tamerlane. Referred to both as the Jewel of Kazakhstan and the Mecca of Central Asia, it is regarded as the most important site of pilgrimage in Kazakhstan, so important in fact, that it is said that three trips to Turkestan were equivalent to the Hajj to Mecca. And given our chances of heading to Mecca (slim), it was clearly going to be an important stop on our sweep through the country. So, despite missing the train, we were determined to get there and this being Central Asia where everyone moonlights as a private driver, were able to rustle up a driver for the four hours round trip.

Not many words were shared between us as we drove the two hours from Shymkent to Turkestan. The highway there cut an almost straight line through flat dusty unremarkable fields. The sky despite being cloudless was an orange haze due to smoke from an unknown source, the sun a pink sphere shining weakly through. It was late lunchtime by the time we arrived and having skipped breakfast and jumped straight into the car, we were hungry enough to eat a horse which we duly proceeded to do. We had arranged a guide to take us through Turkestan, and it was he who met us at lunch and sat and entertained us as we tucked into our equine plov. He was a nice man of roughly our age (33) who had lived in Turkestan his entire life and been a guide for a good portion of it. It was mainly Russians, other Central Asians and a few Americans that he guided, we were his first Australians. He'd also recently married his 16-year-old cousin which he explained very matter of factly, proudly showing us a photo of her. Sated and with the hangover partly subsiding, we paid for lunch and finally got up to see what we'd come for, at which it suddenly dawned on us that neither of us knew exactly what that was. We both knew of the importance of the site, but not what we'd be seeing, so with some confusion and interest, we got up and left.

Following Ismail, we made our way through the empty back streets of Turkestan before suddenly reaching a wide pedestrianised area crowded with pilgrims, the weedy berms becoming replaced by manicured lawns. Stretched out in front of us stood a long crenelated mud-brick wall, with a pathway leading up a set of stairs to its entrance, itself flanked by two guard columns. And sitting in the distance behind the city wall, sat the monuments that made this site so important and impressive. It wasn't the perfectly turquoise blue dome that was designed to juxtapose against the yellow desert, nor the glazed bricks weaving in intricate geometric patterns that adorned the building's exterior. It was simply the sheer scale of them, dwarfing their protective walls.

We walked through the gates, entering a pathway that cut through the earth, so that on either side of us stood a 3-metre-high wall. The enormity of the Khoja Yasawi Mausoleum slowly revealed itself as we approached, emphasised as it stood almost alone in a large field. Its huge face was made entirely of brick, and at each corner sat two large round guard towers themselves flanking the 39-metre-tall monumental entrance. The walls and roof enveloped us as we approached, and walking through a small non-descript door at its base, we stepped into the building's dark cavernous interior, our eyes adjusting as the largest brick dome in Central Asia revealed itself above us. In the centre of the interior sat a large two-tonne ornamental bowl made up of zinc, tin, copper, silver and gold. It had sat here almost without interruption until the Bolsheviks turned up in 1935 and whisked it off to the Hermitage in St Petersburg, only to return it in 1989. We followed our guide through the outer rooms of the structure, passing quietly shuffling pilgrims until we entered a room where many sat, eyes closed while one of them softly chanted.

The structure had been commissioned by Tamerlane in the late 14th century and was the second building he'd built in honour of an Islamic preacher named Ahmed Yasawi, the first sitting next to his own Mausoleum in Samarkand. And in fact, it was the same Ahmed Yasawi that the recently built mosque I'd just witnessed in Astana was also in honour of. This 12th-century Islamic preacher had been born in what would be modern Kazakhstan and was instrumental in spreading Islam across the region. What was particular to Yasawi though was that he preached a version of Islam known as Sufism. An inward-looking version of Islam that rejected worldly goods and the teachings and practises, and adherence to religious hierarchy, and instead promoted Islam as being a personal relationship with oneself and God. And thereby pre-dating Martin Luther by three centuries. It eventually became overwhelmed by more dogmatic versions of Islam, but not before spreading across the world and surviving to the point where 90 million Muslims still follow it. With perhaps the most well-known example being the whirling dervishes of Turkey who spin for hours, placing themselves in a transcendent trance and communication with God. Though given the Sufi's promotion of "love, peace and tolerance"* it has by some logic became a target for many modern extremists, ISIS being but one.

We wandered back outside. Wooden scaffolding protruded from the huge entrance's walls and ceiling above us, owing to the fact that the building had not been completed. When Tamerlane unexpectedly died in 1405, the workers

---

* https://www.nytimes.com/2017/11/24/world/middleeast/sufi-muslim-explainer.html

dropped their tools. Perhaps an indication that this was a Tamerlane glory project that his subordinates had been too afraid to refuse. It is interesting to consider the number of religious structures that Tamerlane did build in his wake, reminding people that he was the "sword of Islam". That the majority of the 17 million people he had murdered were Muslims seemingly didn't matter, though I do like to consider the idea that overwhelming guilt drove him to make amends with his maker. I wonder whether feelings of guilt drove the Kazakh President Nazarbayev to build the largest mosque in Central Asia too. A man whose time as leader has allowed him to become the 9th richest leader on earth* with a wealth that includes a USD$65 million home in London and a USD$63 million castle in Switzerland**. What would Yasawi have said?

We walked across the grounds and looked back as the orange-hued light from a lowering sun settled on the Mausoleum and that of the one standing adjacent to it, its large turquoise dome sitting on top of a drum inscribed with Sufi texts.

*    *    *    *

Wandering before us as we walked back to the car was a young Kazakh couple dressed in their wedding outfits

---

* https://www.thrillist.com/vice/20-richest-world-leaders-ranked-by-net-worth-and-wealth

** https://www.rferl.org/a/qishloq-ovozi-nazarbaevs-wild-kazakhstan-burns/30230218.html

having their photos taken. They waited at the entrance gates for us to pass so that their photographer could grab shots of them as they held each other within the gates, the mausoleum in the background, the low sun casting their long shadows before them. They were conservatively and sweetly dressed, and shyly posed while their photographers snapped away. As we stood there watching, one of their photography crew (which included a videographer, a photographer and a drone operator), became excited and rushed over to our guide. Excited chatter between the photographer and our guide ensued, with them casting nodding glances in our direction. "It would be a great honour for them if you were to bless their wedding", explained my guide. Religiously unreligious and often placing marriage in the same category as the royal family, I hadn't thought myself as necessarily appropriate to be blessing weddings, however, moments later I was standing next to the happy young couple, patting the groom on his back. And telling him and the camera that I wished them all the best, before saying something in Kazakh repeating the words my guide was whispering in my ear. The cameraman clicked away with the three of us earnestly staring into the lens, everything in silence but for a high-pitched buzzing emanating from the drone as it hovered above capturing the confused expression on my face.

Completing my daily wedding blessing, I put my hand on my heart, bowed and said all the best, the newlyweds bowing in return. Turning to my friend, he gave me a bow also, but more in the vein of 'let's move', and so after giving one more protracted goodbye, we left.

\*    \*    \*    \*

Having stuffed myself with vegetables and sparkling water the night before as a sign of penance to my body, I rose more refreshed the following day and set out with my friend to explore Shymkent. It was a rather old city, established in the 12th century as a Silk Road trading hub. But like so many other cities in the region, was destroyed by Genghis Khan and his happy bunch a century later, before being rebuilt under Tamerlane, later incorporated into the 18th century Khanate of Kokhand, followed by the Russian Empire a few decades after that. The etymology of the city's name came from "green, grass", though was clearly born from a different age, as the city was more yellow dust than green, and more pollution spewing traffic clogged streets than grass. Our city map did however show a large park all the more enticing with its little symbol of a pitched tent indicating a circus, so braving the traffic, we set off in search of it.

\*    \*    \*    \*

"Circus open on Nov 5", said the lady behind the counter before beginning to print us both tickets. Sadly though, this was weeks away, and since we didn't intend to fly back for a what I suspected would be a three-hour animal rights abuse show, we had to refuse her tickets. We wandered on ticket-less and stumbled upon a large MIG fighter plan, sitting atop a tall stand. The plane pointed down across the park towards a rather impressive statue memorialising those who had died in the Second World War. Both rather morbid symbols of two wars (The second hot war, and the first cold one), that the Soviets had dragged the Kazakhs into, which they had very little to do with yet were forced to pay dearly for. Illustrating the new materialist present though stood an adjacent Aquapark, but which like the circus was closed. I was later especially disappointed about this fact after having read a highly salacious and titillating, albeit negative, review, pointing out that the park involved 'women with their hair out' and 'men and women swimming together.'

We eventually reached the end of the park, coming across a small exhibition of a local photographer's works. The exhibition was empty but for three traditionally dressed staff behind the ticket booth, who were somewhat startled to see us, presumably as they weren't expecting anyone, let alone foreigners. In a state of shock, they recorded the countries we were from and proceeded to charge us an amount that they couldn't make up their mind about. Seemingly oscillating between ripping us off and giving us a discount, they eventually settled on ripping us off and let us through.

The photos were landscape shots taken around Kazakhstan which to our eyes seemed to be different angles of the same undulating plain. For while Kazakhstan is the 9th largest country on earth and larger than the four other Central Asian countries combined, it is essentially 2.7m square kilometres of dessert and steppe plain. Which is great to raise hordes of horses but not so much for people, and despite its enormous landmass, is home to only 18 million people, ranking it as one of the least dense countries on earth though inching it past Greenland and the Western Sahara. To be fair to the country, along its south-eastern border lay the Tien-Shen Mountain range (and their apples) and to the West, the Caspian Sea. And indeed, adjacent to the Caspian sits the region of Mangistau. A landscape of deep dry depressions, and tall treeless mountains, where the surface seeps a briny water, before it evaporates away in the sun, a landscape who's winter has been compared to that of Norways, and summer to that of Libya's. A harsh, unforgiving region, seemingly devoid of life but for the people manning the refineries and oil rigs that dot this landscape, and a region where our plane from Shymkent was about to deposit us.

# A FORGOTTEN CORNER
# OF ANYWHERE

I had actually learnt of Mangistau through tinder. For a couple of weeks prior to this part of my trip, I'd been speaking to a documentary maker named Ana who like many in the country was of Russian ethnicity but second-generation Kazakh. Unfortunately, Ana pointed out that since we were both adults and that I was simply passing through, meeting up with one another would be a waste of time. Which I thought was very mature (far more than myself), and also a bit of a shame. However, having recently collaborated with the Kazakhstan Tourism Board, she was regardless, eager for me to see the parts of the country 'that tourists haven't yet discovered'. Given that my friends and I and perhaps a smattering of others were the only non-Kazakhs in the country, I thought that was a little rich. Though with the region spanning an area 50% larger than the United Kingdom yet receiving a grand total of 5,000 people a year, it turned out to be spot on. And to really ensure that I received the whole Kazakh Tourism Board experience, she insisted that she would arrange our itinerary and organise our guide. Well hell, why not I thought, so off to Mangistau on the far South-Western corner of Kazakhstan my friend and I went. Which unfortunately meant first landing into Aktau.

# AKTAU AND MANGISTAU

Aktau was established in the 1950s by the Soviet Union after they discovered that this area wasn't only home to inconvenient nomads, but also to extensive deposits of uranium, gas and oil. They built the city in the Soviet style, which is to say in an extremely ugly, formless and soul-sapping way. Viewed from Google Maps, it is ringed by two lakes which would be lovely but for one being coloured bright green and dark black and home to 105 million tonnes of uranium mining waste and the other being a bright pink. With only a day in Aktau before leaving to Manigstau, my friend and I quickly determined that we'd probably booked in about 23 hours too much time here, and moreover, that it was in fact garbage that gave the second lake it's radiant pink. Having eaten a late lunch of a delicious plov, my friend and I decided to explore the city on foot, in the process being accosted by an extremely old and drunk but surprisingly strong man. Walking down a back street, the old man approached us spitting bread between his few teeth as he shouted at us in Russian. Trying to sidestep him, he grabbed me by the arm with an extraordinary grip, clenched his other fist and almost went to swing a punch before I responded in the affirmative to my friend's suggestion of "Shall we run". Thankfully, it wasn't this lovely city that we were in the region for and were being picked up the next morning by our guide.

\*     \*     \*     \*

Our guide and driver was Vladimir, who in the 1980s had moved here from Belarus to work as a nuclear technician at the nuclear power plant that had once powered the cuty. It had operated from 1973 until a lack of funds led to its shutdown in the 90s. With the assistance of the US Department of Energy which had taken the role of safely shutting down aging ex-Soviet nuclear power plants, the plant was finally decommissioned in 1999. Suddenly finding himself without a job, Vladimir became a tour guide which seemed extraordinary to me given 1. The complete lack of tourists and 2. His complete lack of guidance.

But despite being laconic to degree of being almost mute, we managed to determine the plan. We would drive to what had been the lowest dry point in the Soviet Union, bounce our way through desert sand dunes, spend the night next an ancient seabed, continue up into mountain ranges, before returning via an expansive salt plane.

\*  \*  \*  \*

We awoke early that morning to a city that overnight had become covered in a thick blanket of fog which had rolled in off the Caspian Sea. We wandered down to the foyer, met our guide, jumped into his car, and creeped off into the quiet and eerie streets of Aktau. Orange streetlights diffused through the fog which along with our dangerously dim headlamps provided the only available light at which to negotiate the streets.

We were soon at the outskirts of the city amidst an opaque desert landscape dotted with distant jet-black oil refineries. Oil pipelines ran parallel to us as we sped down the highway, often abruptly taking a sharp turn off the ground reaching up and over us and shooting off into the desert to our distant left as we sped underneath.

The sun was now just clear of the horizon and illuminating the fog with a pink hue, silhouetting the distant mixture of scattered industrial infrastructure and broken and abandoned buildings like some Mad-Max dystopic world. I looked at the speedometer which was hovering around 140 km an hour and which seemed incongruous with Vladimir who was sitting forward in his seat peering through the window as if this was all a little unsafe (it was). I soon realised why he was concentrating so hard on driving, not for our safety it turned out, but rather for the sharp turn off to the Karagiye Depression, the once lowest point in the Soviet Union, and the first stop on our itinerary. Unfortunately, the fog hadn't completely cleared and rather than being able to see the full extent of the landscape, we instead saw what looked like islands of landscape peeking through an ocean of cloud.

Onwards we pressed, and with the sun rising and the fog lifting the vast desert plane revealed itself. And as if emerging from the sand a town of perhaps a hundred houses appeared, each one surrounded by tall walls presumably to block out the drifting desert. A single petrol pump and store sat at the town's centre occupied by the only person we saw. And it was here—sadly—that we stopped to buy food provisions for later, which included amongst other things a canned spam-like substance and German waffle biscuits. After filling the car with 15 cents a litre petrol, we continued back into the desert, the town quickly disappearing quickly behind us.

We could sense the landscape was decreasing in elevation and could see to our distant right the long chalky white cliff line of an escarpment. The asphalt road we were on gradually disappeared until it was simply a sandy and stony path, it too eventually giving way to a basic track that cut and bounced us through the sand dunes now surrounding us. These dunes grew higher and steeper so that we began riding them like waves, the horizon coming into and out of view. Everything in the truck including ourselves crashed around us as we drove at pace through this landscape before a particularly hard crash caused Vlad to abruptly stop the truck. For a moment he simply sat there gripping the steering wheel with two hands, blinking through the windscreen, before he cut the ignition and jumped out. "Must be taking a leak", I peered back to say to my mate, though stopped myself short as we both watched Vlad disappear under the truck. We jumped out too, the truck shifting ever so slightly in the sand while perched precariously on an angle with Vlad underneath. We stooped down to see what the problem was. "There… broken", Vlad said to us as he pointed at the sheet of metal that was designed to protect the undercarriage but was now hanging by two of its four corners acting like a shovel to a large pile of sand. Each of us had a go at bending it back into place, but with a lack of tools, and the sheet made of a stiff steel, there was little we could do but to slightly push up one side so at least the vehicle was no longer acting like a snowplough. We all somewhat bitterly recognised that we couldn't carry on, though the conclusion came from Vlad, "We have to turn back". And that we did, 45 minutes of driving in silence to the nearest town which looked rather like an abandoned settlement and would have contained no more than 200 people. Without reception, we drove around this tiny settlement blind, all the more difficult when we discovered that our guide could speak Russian but not Kazakh. And while Russian was the lingua franca for the region, we were in backcountry and it seemed Russian was spoken here only sporadically. Eventually we were directed to a home—a square concrete block with small windows and a corrugated iron roof. And in the front yard, a makeshift pen holding an unlikely trio of a goat, a camel and a horse, all staring at us in silence. A man came out, inspected the car, and without a word disappeared back into his house before reappearing in a one-piece grease-covered blue jumpsuit. Extraordinarily, this miniature town in the middle of nowhere had one auto mechanic and—praise be to Allah—we'd found him. Though either he wasn't particularly fast, the damage was worse than we had considered, or I didn't understand auto-mechanical work (being the most likely option), and so rather than taking the ten minutes I had anticipated, it instead took an hour.

We decided to leave Vlad and the mechanic and went for a walk which 15 minutes later meant had us standing at the town's edge. In the distance was the long line of the chalk escarpment separated from us by a flat unremarkable scrubby plain though punctuated by a single row of ten or so horses walking in our direction. They eventually reached us, a variety of white and brown horses, and slowly made their way past us and onwards into the town behind us. The ground was littered with scrap metal construction miscellanea, and strangely various mismatched shoes. This wasn't a pretty landscape, and it certainly wasn't a pretty town.

We walked back to find Vlad crouched down watching as the man in the overalls banged away at the undercarriage of the truck. A friend of the mechanic had joined and was diligently reaching down and swapping out each tool. From the look of it, he wasn't entirely compos mentis and stared unashamedly at us between assisting with the job, and though while everyone was perfectly friendly, there was a feeling of being in a Kazakh appropriation of the film *Deliverance*.

With a final shrug, the mechanic indicated the repair complete, and paying him a pittance, we jumped back in the truck and shot back out to the dunes, Vlad clearly trying to make up lost time, clearly ignoring the recent lesson.

I felt bad, I'd dragged my mate halfway around the world on the back of a tinder message and here we were in the middle of nowhere bumping up and down along a dirty landscape. I felt bad that was until we cleared the dunes and began to drive at pace no longer on a sandy trail but now simply a flat rock surface, which it soon became apparent was the top of an escarpment overlooking a vast alien landscape. The land below us stretched to the horizon and was marked with giant rock formations reaching out of the ground atop their chalk coloured bases like islands in a flat sea of sand. Which in a sense was partly true as the landscape was—20 million years earlier—a seabed, suspected of once connecting to the ancient Caspian. Vlad dipped the car down a gorge, taking us down from the escarpment before racing along this barren landscape, kicking up a trail of dust that sat still in the air, acting like a marker of where we'd come. Bone white limestone cliffs sat to our right, which eons of erosion had carved into finger-like protrusions that reached across as if gripping the plain. Like the Badlands in the States, rock formations rose from this ancient seabed, the different coloured layers revealing their age.

Turning right and towards the protrusions, Vlad steered between two of the 'fingers' eventually reaching a steep gap in the cliff line, allowing us to ascend to its top. The landscape around us was now rising again, and we drove towards a set of undulating hills before Vlad stopped the car and asked us to follow him on foot. In silent single file we climbed through these hills, the stillness in the air lending the landscape an eery quietness. The steepness petered out as we reached the base of a small long mound and finally, as we reached the top of this last climb, we saw the reason we had been brought here.

We were standing on the flat top of a ridgeline, the lip of an enormous chalky bowl that steeply dropped hundreds of meters towards the desert floor below. The lip of the bowl curved out and around, stretching out across the desert before petering out and sharply eroding itself away. Out in front stood two steeple-like rock formations that made up the 'Valley of Castles'. The top of each 'steeple' was at our eyeline which the low sun was catching and casting their shadows kilometres along the desert plane, itself chalky white as if dusted by frost. Vlad led us around the bowl's edge and across to one corner where the ground had eroded away to the valley floor, leaving a gap a hundred metres across from the first steeple. A crumbling stone structure once used by nomads stood here with us and was whistling in the wind from the chilly breeze sweeping up from the desert. We sat down close to the edge of the bowl and silently contemplated the landscape before us. It all felt so ancient and lifeless, and marked by these megalith seemingly unnatural formations created an acute feeling of otherworldliness. Neither of us spoke, and after some time I turned to see that my friend had closed his eyes and was meditating. The sky was fading from a light blue into an inky purple as the sun, no longer a circle, inched its way over the horizon. Vlad stood up and indicated it was time to go.

We laid out our tents that evening under a limestone bluff, its smooth curved surface worn away by tens of thousands of years of wind. Vlad put together a fire using a liberal dose of kerosene fuel to get it started. Our figures flickered against the white bluff face, as we sat in silence eating our spam and contemplating our isolation amongst this strange landscape. The milky way stretched from one end of the bowl-like sky to the other, undiluted by any artificial light as we, lost in thought, drifted off to sleep.

*    *    *    *

Vlad was already cooking breakfast when we arose—a spam sandwich and a German waffle—which along with a cigarette and a strong coffee we scoffed down before heading for a short walk. The morning sun was casting shadows across the strange landscape and catching scattered rusty metallic globules protruding from the hardened ground. We broke a few of these and threw them into the distance, creating a sound like shattering glass as they broke. In front of us stood a steep cliff with a small clearing where it had crumbled away allowing us to scramble to its top. At its top we found that it was a table with cliffs running around its perimeter until it pinched, allowing for a narrow piece of it to continue and connect to a mesa* in the distance. And on this narrow piece of connecting rock lay the remnants of a stone wall and door frame. Had it been there to hold in livestock, or as a defensive wall we couldn't tell and presumably neither could Vlad who offered us nothing more than "Ancient nomads". He was though referring to the Turkmens who less than 200 years earlier were roaming this land, capturing passing people as slaves and marching them on week-long journeys to the slave towns of Khiva and Bukhara in the east, suggesting that perhaps it may not have been livestock these were designed to keep in.

We were soon driving again, passing only the occasional sign of life in this otherwise sun and wind ravaged landscape. This land was harsh though it soon became harsher as the horizon began to shimmer off a flat white surface spread across the panorama in front of us. The closer we got the more detail we could make out of what was a vast salt flat, made by years of unseen groundwater, evaporating away in the summer heat, leaving behind ever-increasing deposits of salt. We hugged the cliff line to our right to avoid becoming stuck in the gradually thickening surface salt, and eventually right up into them before stopping to have lunch.

Vlad slowly prepared lunch while my friend and I walked out to the salt flat. The ground gradually becoming whiter as we got deeper, until we were amongst tectonic plates of pure salt that folded on one another and crunched under

---

\* An isolated flat-topped high.

our feet. Intense sunlight reflected off the surface, making the landscape all the harsher, though it would catch out pathways underneath the surface that glistened in the sun, giving away the streams seeping from the ground. Our feet sunk into these and broke their salt surfaces, allowing a grey and purple mud to ooze out into our footprints, staining the whiteness of the salt. This landscape felt toxically hostile, and unforgiving to life the only evidence of which was the body of a dead baby duck, its stomach and eyes pecked out, presumably dropped by passing eagles.

We walked back to Vlad and a small lunch of more spam, more instant coffee and more cigarettes. The truck was parked up against the cliff face of a limestone mountain range, formed from millions of years of sitting under a sea. Now like fingers, these cliffs splayed and stretched out across the landscape, each finger carved by the rainfall that fell ever so occasionally. We followed Vlad as he led us through two cliffs converging like a V, to the entrance of a channel that had formed with the walls rounded and smooth. The channel twisted left then right, with debris scattered along the ground, until we reached the end—a wall with a smooth lip at its top, presumably formed by a long since gone river.

My friend put on a podcast for our final journey back across this alien landscape, an interview between Yuvell Noah Harari and Sam Harris, discussing the impact that technology and artificial intelligence were having on our lives. What a juxtaposition to the landscape around me I thought, where ancient burial grounds of once roaming nomads still sat, and where lonely herders lead lines of camels. Though this was broken when after many hours of bumping over this wild terrain, we finally in the distance saw the unmistakable sign of civilisation—tarmac. And finally arriving at it half an hour after seeing it, we met with a highway that took us out of the desert, out of the wild and back into the beautiful form of civilisation, Aktau.

*    *    *    *

We had two hours free in Aktau before leaving and walked down to the newly developed walkway that took us along the Caspian Sea. This Sea was once considered by the Ancient Greeks to have been part of the ocean that they thought ringed the world, giving Alexander the Great the impression, after arriving on the Iranian shores, that he was standing at the edge of the world. Today, whether it is even a sea or a lake, is up for debate. It *is* the largest inland body of water in the world, *and* is salty, albeit a third of that of the Mediterranean, but it is also home to 90% of the world's caviar producing sturgeon and perhaps more significantly 50 billion barrels of oil. Were it to be a lake, the Caspian would be shared evenly between the five countries ringing it, if instead a sea, then proportional to their shorelines. In the end, it was—politically—impossible to determine, though an agreement was reached that it would at least no longer be militarised. Which was quite a change for Russia who for the past 300 years *has* militarised it, and indeed it was the Caspian that allowed them to subjugate the Central

Asia Khans. Just north of Aktau, for instance, stands Fort Shevchenko, established in 1846 as part of their push east, and further south, Fort Krasnovodosk where the Russian military arrived before marching inland and capturing Khiva. Years later, this latter fort became a gateway to the gulags, where swept up in Stalin's purges, the intelligentsia, Kulaks and other unwanted Soviet detritus were shipped to before being loaded onto trains and sent deep into Central Asia.

While we wouldn't be packed into trains, and hadn't yet been caught for our crimes against the state, standing here on the edge of Central Asia, we too were about to turn away from the Caspian and head back, deep into Central Asia.

# UZBEKISTAN

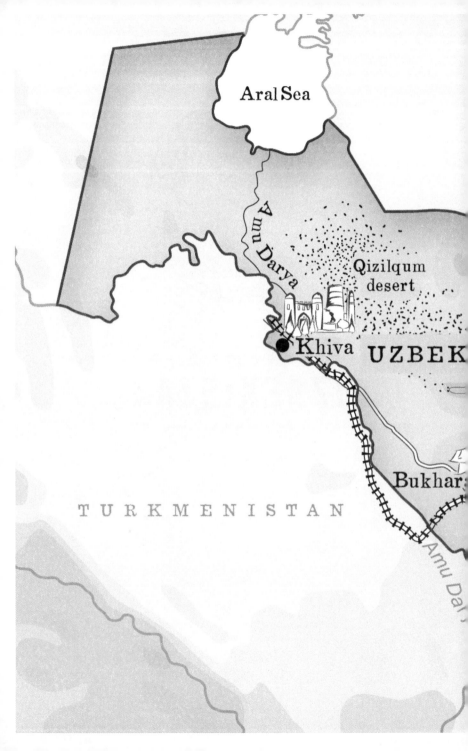

AZAKHSTAN
N
Aydar Lake
Tashkent
Ugam-Chatkal National Park
markand
KYRGYSTAN
TAJIKISTAN

N othing could save us from the ferociousness of the man-selling Uzbeks, the country, the people, everything was bad", wrote Alexander Burns.

I had been reading Alexander Burn's book *Travels into Bokhara*, in which he describes his clandestine trip through Central Asia on behalf of the British Empire in 1835. It had been an instant best-seller, had propelled him to fame and led to a promotion that soon sent him to Afghanistan to negotiate a treaty on behalf of the British Government, where he was duly murdered. His initial trip had taken him through the lands of the Khanates where he firsthand mingled with the Uzbeks, a people he didn't take particularly well too. Reading this, not to mention several other people's accounts of the region, had me wondering how they could be so different from the Kazakhs. But for the people of Kara Dala (who I now strongly suspect had manipulated their Google Rating), I had found the Kazakhs to be warm, friendly and engaging. Sharing a 2,300 km long border, and a good portion of their history, I imagined that the Uzbeks would be much the same. And now sitting on a plane on a flight to Tashkent, Uzbekistan's capital, I came across my first examples. Billowing across the two seats in front of me for instance, was the largest man in Central Asia and to his right two of perhaps the most thuggish. The three of whom made for an excellent example of why the Uzbek habit of attempting to empty the overhead bins of your bags and make your way to the front as soon as the screech of the wheel hit the tarmac, was such a bad idea. Squeezed out of the plane like toothpaste, Andrew and I made our way to customs where the customs box for people needing visas was empty. Waiting an hour while everyone around us were quickly processed, two slovenly looking blokes finally approached and proceeded to compete for the prize for processing a visa with the least amount of manners in the slowest amount of time. "Come!" barked the man to me without bothering to look up.

My first impressions of the Uzbeks were not good but then you can hardly judge a population of 30 million from a single plane flight—imagine judging the 25 million Australians on a flight from Bali to Brisbane for example. No, the judgement would come later. We were now in Tashkent at the start of this leg of the trip that would take us from Tashkent (the capital) to Samarkand (the 'Taj Mahal of Central Asia'), to Bukhara ('The Eastern Dome of Islam') and finally to Khiva ('the slave-trading capital of Central Asia'*).

---

*    I believe it no longer retains this name.

# TASHKENT

Having made our way through customs, seemingly to the displeasure of the border guards, we pushed out through the throngs of people that met every airport and train station arrival in Central Asia and exited out into the sun. We had arrived into Tashkent, home to two and a half million Uzbek citizens making it Central Asia's largest city, in what was Central Asia's most populous country.

Tashkent hadn't always held this distinction and for much of its history had instead been rather inconsequential. For 1,000 years, it had sat as a small town in what is now known as the Tashkent Oasis while the city's neighbours saw all the action. Alexander the Great had ignored it despite both establishing Khujand a mere 120 km south and conquering Samarkand just beyond that. And even after being absorbed into the Kingdom he left behind, it sat languishing for another entire millennia before gaining any prominence. Though with the arrival of the Arab armies in the 8th century this began to change. For as they swept away the feuding powers, replacing them with the homogeneity of their own, the Silk Road re-emerged which Tashkent then capitalised on. So much so that within 500 years, it had become one of the larger and more influential cities in the region, even catching the eye of the 'The Great Khan' who in 1220 turned up and proceeded to destroy it. Tamerlane took a different view to his ancestor and during his reign in the late 14th century set about reconstructing it, allowing it to return to prosperity again. From then on it became the property of the Uzbeks. First the Khan of Bukhara, later the Khan of Kokand before climbing greatly in prominence after becoming the capital of Russian Turkestan in 1865, the capital of the Uzbek Soviet Socialist Republic in 1929, and finally the capital of modern Uzbekistan in 1992.

It was after becoming the capital of Russian Turkestan though that saw it rise in the eyes of the West, which in turn attracted explorers and adventures. All of whom seemed to regard the place as rather dangerous.

"I had scarcely closed my eyes when I awoke to find my neighbours on each side shaking me and asking me in agitated tones whether I realised that I'd fallen asleep. On replying that that was what I was trying to do, they seemed profoundly shocked and explained that if you were foolish enough to go to sleep out of doors in a city like Tashkent then anything might happen to you", described Fitzroy Maclean on his journey through the city. While I couldn't confidently say for Andrew, I could at least say for myself that I didn't intend to sleep on any park benches, and of course, that was from 1937, surely the tides of progress had changed things. "Uzbekistan and its capital are one of the least safe countries in the world I have visited. One night after spending many hours in a night club, and without any result, I came out to take a taxi to my hotel. The taxi driver took me to a quiet place and stole all my money and left me in the street…" wrote a TripAdvisor Review. Bugger it, we thought, we'd just have to keep our wits about us, avoid sleeping on benches and late nights in nightclubs, neither of which were high up our list of priorities.

Our most immediate priority at this point was to eat, so having weaved our way through the traffic of the city, we arrived at the hotel, dumped our bags and went straight out into the Tashkent Streets. Thankfully we didn't have to interrupt our search for food by checking in with the local police station as our hotel was able to complete our 'registration'. Had we booked an Airbnb or hostel, we would've been obliged to register with the local police station—itself a recipe for exploitation—or face potential deportation. And we would have to ensure that from this point on in Uzbekistan, we registered at every place we stayed so that we could officially account for our trip through the country when we were being processed by customs on the way out. All a hangover from the Soviet days when neurotic paranoia reached a fever pitch. My concern wasn't so much deportation—it would've made for a good anecdote frankly—or paying a bribe, which surely couldn't have been much. It was more having to deal with the incompetence of the customs and falling into some Kafkaesque nightmare. Either way, we were in the safe hands of our friendly hotel receptionist, and having arranged our registration, headed straight for lunch, to what seemed to be the Must Do of Tashkent—*The Plov Centre.*

*   *   *   *

*Plov,* the national dish *and* national obsession of Uzbekistan. Made from a mixture of oily rice, sliced carrots, onion, quail eggs and horse, it is inexpensive, served everywhere and completely delicious. And what better place for us to try this than the Plov Centre, a football-sized site with a restaurant for a few hundred at one end, and at the other a large concrete ground with large stone cauldrons cooking over open fire pits, being stirred by old babushkas sweating into them presumably to enhance the flavour.

Grabbing a plate and some greasy cutlery, we joined the queue which seemed to grow as quickly in front of us as it did behind us as people shoved and pushed their way in. Finally making it to the front of the line where we held up our plate to the chef as if in a Dicken's plot, the hairy fat chef wearing a singlet and—unnecessarily in my view—a chef's hat, scooped up some rice, threw it down on our plate and began serving the people behind us. Pointing out to him that our plates lacked the primary ingredients of a Plov being both meat and quail eggs, in some irritation the Chef plopped a small amount of each on our plates and pushed us along. "What a rude bastard", I said to Andrew, followed by "What a rude bitch", as the first person I approached to ask where we were to sit simply brushed me aside and walked off. We worked it out eventually though. As a foreigner what you do is this. First, you line-up and allow others to push in front of you. You then wait patiently to watch others get served conspicuously more than you. Following this, you enter the restaurant in order to be ripped off in front of a seemingly in-on-it crowd by the people serving the salads and drinks. At this point, you are welcome to ask for assistance to what appears to be people working there but are actually apparitions. And finally, you assist any other person who looks non-Uzbek and who is undoubtedly being conned. "Authentic experience" was the title of a review I'd read about the Plov Centre, and even this early on in my Uzbek experience, I was starting to think that yes, perhaps this would be the authentic experience of the country.

\*    \*    \*    \*

"Have you had plov yet? We will see you tonight at your hotel at 630", the message from my Tashkent mate had read. Because against all odds, I had a contact in Tashkent. A very distant one to be sure the friend of the business partner of a friend of mine in Sydney—but a local contact, nonetheless. And so at 6.30pm, Andrew and I were picked up by Ben and Shakhruz. "Whatever we do, don't let them take us to a nightclub", Andrew had insisted. I couldn't have agreed with him more, not only am I not a nightclub type bloke, everything I'd read about them sounded horrendous. Take this TripAdvisor review for instance:

> *"Night life is dead and dangerous in Tashkent and is in the hand of mafia, and police. The girls you may find in the clubs are mainly prostitutes which are already completely spoiled in Dubai or other international capitals".*

Thankfully that review was from 2006, and the mafia problem had since been solved. The recently deceased and first President of Uzbekistan—Islam Karimov—had convened a meeting with the local heads of crime to once and for all divvy up control of the drug trade, and with them all in one place simply had them shot. Either way, it wasn't the mafia or the 'spoiled prostitutes' that turned us off nightclubs, it was because we were somewhat stodgy with our ability to dance being limited by our British heritage. "Tonight, we have dinner, we go to my office to smoke joints with my friend… and then we go to nightclub", "Sounds great", my friend and I chimed in unison.

The first part of the night did actually sound good. "If you want to travel in peace, you must howl like the wolves among whom you find yourself", a French explorer had suggested to the 19th century Alexander Burns as he travelled through the region*. Being both humans who needed dinner, and

---

* Which would arguably be the equivalent of saying 'When in Rome…'

millennials who liked joints, we were ready to howl. And perhaps being fed with food and cannabis would make the second part of the night enjoyable.

The restaurant chosen was an Irish Pub which in any other instance would've been a little disappointing, but having spent considerable time eating often questionable food, something familiar sounded good. Especially given the luxury of being able to smoke indoors.

Both of these blokes had lived outside of Uzbekistan for at least a decade, Ben having lived in Australia and Shakruz in Russia and the USA. And it was this that gave them a unique view of Uzbekistan's place in the world, and the significant changes that were now taking place following the death of President Karimov.

As with each of the modern Central Asian countries, Karimov had been the leader of his country on either side of the date of Independence from the USSR. And like the other leaders, had enforced this continuous rule with a strong hand. With a civil war breaking out in neighbouring Tajikistan almost as soon as the USSR dissolved, Karimov used this as a pretence for cracking down hard on opposition and society in general. After a wave of car bombings in Tashkent in 1999, Karimov had said, "I am ready to rip the heads off 200 people, to sacrifice their lives, for the sake of peace and tranquillity in this country. If a child of mine chooses such a path, I myself would rip off his head". Initially accepted by the population as the lesser of two evils, where the population was willing to exchange personal liberty for personal safety, the public's acceptance of him started waning as the second and then third decade rolled around. His two daughters, Lola and Gulnara Karimova became very conspicuous displays of the nepotism and corruption of his rule. Lola flitting around the world, attending society events, always fashionably dressed, face frozen and ageless*. But it was Gulnara that really represented corruption at its core, as she bullied her way into any business that made money whether it was in telecommunications or healthcare. At least five times I heard her referred to by various people we met as "that bitch", and in one restaurant in Bukhara, the menu displayed the Gulnara Kebab which as the image on the menu showed was a bed of rice containing a face made of pieces of carrot, with pieces of meat skewered through it as the limbs. It escalated to the point when in 2015 she was placed under house arrest, even while her father was still in power. Her whereabouts today is unknown and various reports have her dying of food poisoning or being locked away in prison.

It seemed though, speaking with these blokes, that with the death of Karimov, Uzbekistan was undergoing a renaissance. Relations with Uzbekistan's Central Asian neighbours were being purposefully restored, doors were being opened to foreign investment and restrictions on freedom of information and speech were being reduced. Perhaps most significantly for the Uzbeks though was the ending of what had been referred to by foreign observers as an appalling display

---

\* See Lola's Instagram here: @lola_tillyaeva

of forced labour. For Stalin had designated Uzbekistan as the USSR's cotton-growing region, which meant at one point the country was producing 70% of the Soviet Union's cotton! And to harvest this labour-intensive crop, entire swathes of the Uzbek population—whether they were cleaners, teachers or doctors—were conscripted twice a year to pick cotton for weeks at a time. A practise that had been shockingly enforced up until essentially now.

"Ok so now go to my office to smoke weed", Ben said after a heavy draw on his cigarette. "My friend is bringing it around, but there's something you must know… he's actually a policeman, but he's a good one", he said frankly, presumably good one meaning a bad one. Or a good bad one perhaps. Soon enough we were back in his office as the policeman and his mate, a bloke that was a spitting image of Mr. Bean, turned up. The policeman himself looked rather unusual too, with an age of either 22 or 45, covered in freckles and a mop of copper-red hair. Neither speaking a lick of English, they gesticulated wildly to express how happy they were that we were in their country, before proceeding to confirm that by sitting down and forming a professional factory line of joint creation. Which along with the Frangelico and milk being freely poured, all got us rather liberated. Though as this Central Asian bacchanalia reached its crescendo, it was determined that it was time to head out and so piling into the cop's car, with Mr. Bean heading home, we sped off to the clubs.

*   *   *   *

A bar was the first place we went to, the gaudy grand entrance hiding the fact that its interior was simply a room with a bar at one end, a dance floor in the middle, and some tacky faux leather seating at the other. Tragically, on a mezzanine above the bar was the DJ who looked roughly about 18 with an area behind him representing some sort of VIP area, that was clearly filled with his young friends—all male. Thankfully, this being Central Asia, the drinks were criminally inexpensive and you could smoke everywhere so at least we were able to watch this tragedy that small-time bars so often are, unfold in front of us while feeding ourselves with booze and tobacco. Bunches of girls standing in tight circles danced with one another on the area that had been designated the dance floor, while groups of young men sat in equally tight circles and stared from their chairs. And strangely amongst all of this appeared a dancing teddy bear. The size of a child, with a smiling teddy bear head, and a rather tight outfit, this teddy bear costume was—we determined—occupied by a midget. And a midget with surprisingly good dance moves. But for us, no one found this extraordinary, as the midget in the bear suit weaved his or her way around the dancers on the floors, dropping ergonomically inventive moves. "I actually don't come here often, or really go out at all anymore", Ben said somewhat self-consciously, "So, I think we go to the next club, it's very exclusive, you see all the local celebrities there", he carried on to our dismay. And so, jumping up from the bar, we beelined for the exit, narrowly avoiding the teddy bear who had since spotted us and as was jigging its way in our direction.

We made our way to the car of the cop, as he would be driving us to our next destination, surprising to me at the time given that we'd been drinking steadily and that he was a policeman of the law. Little matter though as we were soon speeding down the highway with myself in shotgun. Discovering that we were heading in the wrong direction, the cop pulled a sharp U-turn, crossing the highway onto the road coming the other way, where we were duly and immediately met with the sirens of a police car and pulled over. Our police friend swiftly parked, grabbed documents from his glove box and jumped out to meet the approaching officer. We couldn't see much but for the two figures seemingly in negotiation, before our guy jumped back in and was about to put his documents back in the glove box, but before doing so flashed his police badge at me and with a wink said the only words I'd heard him speak in English, "Special Passport".

We arrived at the club, the entrance flanked by two block-headed man giants who allowed us to pay the entrance fee of a few dollars and let us enter. The music was comically and uncomfortably loud. Screaming at one another, we made our way to a booth and ordered a round of drinks. Not being able to talk, we sat, stoically drinking cheap Central Asia beer while our brains were steadily mashed by the pulsating shock therapy of the speakers. Ben was screaming at me from across the table, which after squinting and thereby focusing my eyesight I was able to properly hear him suggest we head out the back where there is a quieter, nicer area. I continued to squint but now more for myself as I inwardly wondered why we were permanently damaging our hearing when there was a known alternative. We walked the length of the club, girls sitting alone sipping on a drink glaring at us as we walked past, presumably some of those non-prostitutes that the ancient Romans had referred to. Opening a glass door, we entered what by comparison was a luxuriously peaceful room and made our way to a large comfortable booth. A waiter was at our table immediately, with Ben taking over and ordering a bottle of vodka and—strangely—a plate of fruit. Plates of fruit seemed to be the done thing as the tables of people around us all had plates of fruit in front of them too. It was actually an excellent idea, after eating stodgy pub food followed by cigarettes and alcohol, a plate of fresh and rather exotic fruit went down like a treat. A man approached our table to introduce himself. He was the owner and wanted to personally welcome Andrew and I to his club and threw in another plate of fruit on the house. It eventually and thankfully came time to pay, which is when our friends pulled out their purses.

Inflation in the country had steadily eroded the value of the currency so that one Uzbeki som now equalled 0.0001 USD. What that meant was that the 1 Uzbeki som notes up to the 100 Uzbeki som notes were in our circumstances almost useless, and instead, we'd often paid with the 1,000,

10,000 and 50,000 Uzbeki notes, with the latter being the highest denomination and equal to roughly USD$6. And since most places didn't accept credit cards, it always resulted in people carrying significant amounts of cash on them. And the best place to store that much cash was a purse. What's more, with so much cash circulating between people, almost everyone we encountered in Uzbekistan was extremely adept at counting money. Every transaction, whether it was a pack of cigarettes or dinner resulted in the cashier counting money as if we had just made some large illegal drug transaction. What this meant for us in the immediate circumstance—where we were tallying up a bill of four blokes who had sat in a club for over an hour ordering drinks, cigarettes and fruit—was that between us we needed almost 400 x 10,000 notes, even despite the fruit plate on the house.

*    *    *    *

We arose sheepishly the following morning, both feeling somewhat unwell which I could only blame on the fruit. We were done with drinking and were done with clubs—that was until we weren't done with them of course. Our first stop this morning would be the Chorsu Bazaar, known as the largest bazaar in Central Asia though a title that I was under the growing impression was rather fluid. We decided walking there would offer us some much-needed exercise and so rising early, we set off through the quiet streets of Tashkent.

Close to our hotel we arrived first at the Amir Timur (Tamerlane) square, sitting at the city's centre, with a large strident statue of Tamerlane on a horse and the words engraved in the plinth "Power is in Justice". Here was a man whom one could argue was the most appallingly violent in the history of humanity, who not only murdered his victims but would have children trampled to death by his cavalry, millions of others beheaded and raped. Who would destroy his victim's cities so thoroughly that they never recovered, often sowing barley where once the city had stood, thereby ensuring its removal from the Earth. And who inflicted so much agony and misery on such a large portion of the world, that he was single handidly responsible for wiping out 5% of the world's population. "That which Amir Temur valued most—well-being, prosperity and, above all else, peace and harmony", was how one member of the Uzbek Academy of Sciences wrote. For while he may be regarded by most as evil reincarnate, for the nation of Uzbekistan he had now been put forward as their founder. No problem that he wasn't actually Uzbek.

In front of Tamerlane's statue sat Hotel Uzbekistan, with its brutalist façade representing one faded example of 1970s Soviet modernist architecture. It was a rather legendary hotel that had once serviced the USSR powerbrokers, though the day we entered its foyer the lights were switched off to save on power, the ATMs were out of order and the hotel was only accepting Uzbek couples that could produce a marriage certificate. No power, no money and no fornication, surely a regression from the days of their Russian overlords.

We carried onwards, through quiet city parks, before stumbling upon "Tashkent City", an immense multi-billion-dollar

80-hectare redevelopment of the city centre. It was spear-headed by the new President who, like a modern-day Haussmann, was forcefully demolishing the ancient parts of the city and replacing them with his vision. Labelled by critics as "Dictator Chic", it will eventually be a collection of glass and steel buildings, designed to showcase the new country to foreign investors. And for reasons that allude me, Mike Tyson was chosen to be the celebrity front for this project, whose tattooed smiling face was now looking down on us from the billboards above.

And juxtaposed against Mike Tyson's broad smile, was the Ko'Kaldosh Madrassa, an ornate madrassa built in the 16ᵗʰ century which heralded the start of the Chorsu Bazaar. After taking a quick detour and investigation of the madrassa, whose internal coves contained various workman producing trinkets, we arrived at the outer zone of the Bazaar. People swarmed everywhere, smoke rose from makeshift BBQs manned always by men, and mats littered the floor, splayed out with whatever the shouting women from behind it had to offer. In the hazy distance, we could see the centre of the Bazaar, a large blue dome that represented the inner part of the market, separated from us by swirling masses of colourfully dressed people.

We pushed our way through the crowds while being shouted at by people trying to sell us things that we did not need. As we ventured deeper, the Chinese electronics made way first to a ring of stalls selling nuts from enormous sacks, and then to the fruits, themselves stacked in pyramids a person high. Passing these too with the air becoming more viscous, we reached the blue dome itself, its round roof covering one large open butcher, producing an overwhelming smell. We felt slightly like we were intruding as we pushed our way past the negotiating people, and with it dawning on us that this would not be the time to try horse offal, made our way back out into the relative freshness of the fruit stands.

I was purchasing an—in hindsight—excessive amount of dried fruit, when a young boy wearing a fez hat ran up to us and in broken English told us to follow him to the stall selling carpets. Andrew was in fact in the market for a carpet and was willing to pay anything for the right one, something in reflection would've been prudent for me not to have mentioned. The boy led us at a steady pace through the rings of the market, weaving us between the stalls until we reached the entrance of a hallway built into the market building itself. We followed the boy in, eventually arriving at a windowless room piled high at each end with rolled carpets and a carpet seller who jumped up from a chair to greet us. At this point it dawned on me that in the past half hour I'd absent-mindedly eaten 15 apricots which I now realised would be forming a rather cement-like plug in my internal system and was making me rather sluggish. So, finding a chair in the corner, I sat down to watch as my friend negotiated his way to a carpet.

The carpets the seller produced were indeed very beautiful, with each carpet expressing the many months and sometimes years that the carpet weavers would laboriously design, weave, clip, dye and then wash each one to fruition. There was richness in the detail, each carpet with its own slight imperfections or variation coming from the variation and imperfection of each carpet maker, something a machine would find hard to imitate. One after the other, a carpet was unfurled by the seller who would grab a corner and expertly cast it across the room, the pile growing larger as Andrew rejected each one. Eventually a carpet was rolled out that caught Andrew's eye, a beautiful carpet with colourful rectangles forming the outer border, and intricate geometric patterns making up its centre, the thickness and slight sheen giving it a feeling of quality. We both agreed that this was perfect, at which point the negotiations started.

The carpet seller started proceedings by confidently throwing out a figure that sounded perfectly reasonable to me, but judging by the mock horror of Andrew, not to him. In a quick-fire response, Andrew shot back with a price that caused both the seller and I to recoil. I ate my 16th apricot and waited for the reply. The seller scoffed and appealed to the boy who had led us to the room, before eventually coming up with a number slightly lower than his first. Andrew simply shook his head and got up to leave, motioning for me to follow. "Ok!" Shouted the seller, lowering his price further. I looked to him and then to Andrew, slowly mouthing another apricot. Andrew looked him in the eyes and shook his head before carrying on down the hallway. We were halfway down the hall when the seller appeared from the room and shouted a price lower than the last. Andrew turned around and raised his eyebrows as if to say, *that's the best you can do?* The seller was silent for a moment and presumably finally accounting for the fact that we weren't as wealthy as we first appeared, in a sigh of resignation, stated what surely must've been his final price. Andrew looked at me with a nod, and with a big smile walked across to shake the hand of the seller whose face was already erupting into a barely concealed grin. The tension was immediately diffused, and we all got down and chipped in to help roll up and package the carpet. That all parties were happy seemed to indicate a fair price had been reached, and I later understood that the theatrics were all part of the process. For me, however, who has the uncanny ability of creating awkwardness while at the same time being completely averse to it (probably related), haggling did not come naturally. I'd rather an inflated fixed price any day.

*     *     *     *

We had one day left in Tashkent and decided to take the advice of our friends and head to the mountains in the East. Their recommendation had been a vague "head to the mountains, they're great", and we failed when trying to explain it to our hotel receptionist who was booking us a driver, exactly what we wanted to see. The driver she rustled up, though not being able to speak English, seemed to drive with purpose, and indeed seemed to be racing through traffic to get us somewhere, so we left it to him.

We headed east, along a road running adjacent to a river pouring down from the mountains for about an hour before taking a sharp right up an into them. The ancient engine of our driver's car increased its pitch as it strained against the steepness of what I had to say was a reasonably gentle gradient. The roads around us were empty and the mountain landscape somewhat bare, which contrasted nicely the scene we came across as we rounded a bend arriving into what seemed to be a mass car boot sale. Traditionally dressed Uzbeks roamed amongst the parked cars, peering into what each car owner was selling in this seemingly ad hoc open-air market.

Our driver parked the car amongst the commotion and motioned for us to walk towards a single-story building buttressed against the hill, that happened to be the base of a cable car that was shooting people off in pairs up the mountain. We dutifully joined the queue, attracting considerable attention by being the only non-Uzbeks in the crowd and before we knew it, were launched with a lurch up the mountain on a wooden rickety swing. The swing swayed aggressively as we ascended, thankfully not advertising the fact it had been built by the Soviets decades earlier. We soon arrived to a bare clearing on the mountain and a smattering of people wandering around in groups. A man to our right was giving people rides on his horse and a babushka to our left was sitting on a chair with hundreds of *Kurts* laid out in front of her. Kurts being small hardened sour cheese balls made from the milk of a mare, perfect for Central Asian nomads who had used them for centuries as easily preserved long-distance snacks.

The view swept back down the mountain and across to the planes that stretched out and surrounded Tashkent in the distance. Those planes spread south across Uzbekistan and Turkmenistan, unimpeded by any major geographical barrier, all the way to the border of Iran. And equally to the north, a single flat expanse spreading thousands of kilometres across Uzbekistan and Kazakhstan, to the border and forests of Russia. It has been remarked that it was this enormous flat expanse offering no natural geological protection, that had allowed invaders to simply sweep across, something that Alexander the Great, the Arab armies, Genghis Khan and his Golden Horde, Tamerlane and later the Russians and then Soviets all easily did.

Above us stretched the rest of the mountain, and feeling in need of some exertion, we decided to climb to its top. There was no path, and the mountain was steep and craggy giving a slight feeling of uneasiness as we climbed, particularly as we passed a recently placed memorial to a girl implying that she'd died on that spot.

We eventually reached the top to find an old radar station, the windows of which were broken and the red paint of the big solid balloon containing the radar dish chipped away and faded. Stretched out before us lay the national park and the mountain range that ran through it and into Kyrgyzstan sitting a mere 17 km away. Despite later discovering that the chair lift we had taken operated in the middle of winter as a ski lift, up here above that point, it felt as if no one had been here for years. No one to inspect the presumed Soviet-era military relic that was slowly rusting and falling apart, one of surely many scattered across this vast ex-Soviet empire.

Back at the base we found our driver haggling over some dried fruits though he gave this up when he saw us and went and fetched the car. I offered him the kurts, but he shook his head with a scrunched-up face, clearly sharing our view of the sour chalky little balls.

We rose through the tightly packed mountains that obscured our view before they opened up and gave us a spectacular view across the Soviet-built Chavrak Reservoir in the distance below us. High up from this angle, we could make out boats and yachts cruising their way around this huge man-made lake, and the odd hotel dotting its shoreline. Three retro-futuristic green triangles stood out amongst the rest and sat upon a symmetrically divided plot, which turned out to have once been a Soviet health resort. One of many that had once been dotted across the Soviet Union, designed to service the needs of the Soviet worker who after months of service to the good of the Union, would be sent here to recuperate (unlike in the decadent West where people went on holiday to travel or god forbid, relax). I would go on to experience this recuperation first hand, which amongst other things involved cleaning of my bowels via a mechanical chair, but that would be weeks later, and in Tajikistan.

The road carried us down towards the lake, giving our car's engine a much-needed respite, and brought us to the town of Chorvoq sitting at the point where the Lake was pouring through the gates of the dam and down the valley towards Tashkent. Our driver parked the car and motioned for us to follow him, where he took us to a charming little restaurant for a late afternoon lunch. Ordering our daily plov, we sat cross-legged on the comfortable raised platform, amongst groups of lively Uzbeks at their own platforms, wiling away their Sunday afternoon. Small rocky streams ran between each platform, and heavy old trees towered above us filtering dappled sunlight down onto our table. Alexander the Great was said to have passed by this exact spot ~2,400 years earlier, claimed the restaurant, and before that, a group of Neanderthals evidenced by the petroglyphs in the hills above us.

*    *    *    *

It was evening by the time we arrived back to Tashkent and were dropped to the Tashkent train station with our driver giving us a friendly wave before his car coughed out some exhaust and spluttered off into the traffic. We turned to the station, a somewhat grand building that captured both a Soviet and an Islamic style, particularly the former when we considered the concerningly large security presence who rummaged through our bags before coldly waving us in.

Using our bags as seats, we waited for our high-speed train, a train that along with a new high-speed train network had been built in 2011 for the outrageously cheap price of USD$70 million. What once had taken a good part of a day along the Russian Empire-built 'devil's wagon' line, would now take two hours on a high-speed Spanish one. And for the price of USD$20 each we didn't even have to sit with the proletariat but rather the bourgeoise and Kulaks up in First Class. "Warm towel Sir", asked the waitress as our train sped at 250 km/h to Samarkand—the 'Taj Mahal of Central Asia'.

# SAMARKAND

I t was night-time by the time we arrived into Samarkand's train station, and but for the aggressive barking of a few hidden dogs, the place was entirely quiet. An Uzbek businessman who'd been eyeing us suspiciously had seized his chance and struck up a conversation just as we were pulling into the station. Rather than being suspect, which was my initial assumption after being surreptitiously glanced at for two hours, he turned out to be amiable and curious. Uncertain about the honesty of his brethren, he guided us across to the waiting taxis where he told a driver in what sounded like fairly stern words where to take us, before telling the cost and said with a wagging finger, "not to let him charge a Som more".

Fifteen minutes later, we arrived at our hotel, a small three-storey building behind a high perimeter gate opening onto an alley that was completely dark but for the glow of a single orange streetlight. We knocked at the ancient iron gates initially to silence until we heard the light patter of footsteps. The gate creaked open ever so slightly and the head of a miniature, but entirely normally proportioned man peered out, looked us up and down and beckoned us in. We stepped through the gate and into a tiled courtyard, following the *Homo Floresiensis*-like man in front of us, around the lush overgrown garden at the courtyard's centre, and into the foyer to check in. It was late and we had already eaten so rather than heading for our night-time allotment of Plov, we instead headed to the rooftop balcony, bottle of wine in hand.

The night was cool and still, and the light of a star-filled sky draped over the ancient grounds of Samarkand that stretched away in front of us. Spotlights were elegantly bathing a turquoise dome to our distant left, part of a mausoleum built by Tamerlane almost 700 years earlier. And to our right stood the Mausoleum of Tamerlane himself, its radiant dome slightly misshapen and missing a few tiles, divulging the centuries that had passed since its construction. In front of the dome stood two columns, with ground lights casting a shadowy light which captured the geometric blue and gold patterns that twisted their way up. While the city was as old as many others, had been sacked, and conquered by tyrants for millennia, it was Tamerlane that it became synonymous with and he with it. For Samarkand was his child, his life-long project that in order to build, he had the whole known world destroyed. "Let he who doubts our power, look upon our buildings", he said. And since he saw himself as the most important person on Earth, ordained by God, he needed a capital that reflected that. Like the Great Pyramids, tens of thousands of slaves were wielded by an omnipotent despot to construct buildings of precedent-setting magnitude. And to Tamerlane, the importance of size was only matched by the importance of beauty, and along with the architects that he spared in the destruction of rival cities, so too were spared the stonemasons and artisans, glass blowers and potters. All of whom were marched back from their ruined cities to Samarkand, so many—it was said—that the city was not big enough to hold them all. They were of course still war booty and treated as such. Returning from campaigns, Tamerlane on seeing his project not yet complete would often explode into rages, ordering the sites torn down and the architects publicly hanged. The result was buildings unrivalled in the region, and that would remain unrivalled until perhaps two centuries later with the construction of the Taj Mahal to Samarkand's South. That the ruler who built *that* monument was a direct descendant of Tamerlane, is perhaps no surprise. Nor that it was rumoured he had the worker's hands cut off following its completion.

*   *   *   *

We woke early the following morning and set out for a jog just as the city was rousing. Quietly closing the iron gate behind us, we jogged to the Amir Temur Park that was empty but for a single campervan covered in bumper stickers including—I thought incredibly—a number indicating its New Zealand origin. The buildings we had admired the night before sat alone catching the morning sun. A glorious statue of Tamerlane sat next to the park, sitting at the centre of an empty roundabout, throned, robed and crowned, his hands resting on his sword. His gaze was fixed along Registan Street, Samarkand's most important road connecting its most important buildings, and a road that he had built. We followed this ancient road up, jogging past café workers slowly setting out chairs, but who stopped and stared as we went past. And then gradually as we ascended the hill that postcard view of Central Asia came into being, for before us was the Registan.

*    *    *    *

"The noblest public square in the world", described George Curzon, the late 19<sup>th</sup> century Viceroy* of India. This square—the Registan—has for centuries been captured in paintings and drawings and has long represented the romance of Central Asia. A large rectangular patterned stone courtyard makes up its centre, with three ostentatiously decorated madrassahs opening onto it, each flanked by tall columns complimenting their entrances. For much of history, it was the site of a marketplace, where merchants travelling the

---

* A title given to the Governor Generals of India during the British Raj meaning Governor General.

Silk Road would trade their alien produce while their camels were stationed in the surrounding caravanserais. It was Tamerlane's grandson the 'Astronomer-king' Ulugh Beg who built this, but without the architectural talent Tamerlane had brought by force to the city, it could not have existed.

It was no longer functioning as a marketplace, and as we stood there that morning, at the top of marble steps stepping down to the courtyard, the only occupants were two security guards sitting on steps sharing a cigarette, dwarfed by the madrassah above them. Its columns cast long shadows across the courtyard, catching the morning light, and the glazed tiles making up the Madrassah's portals glistened with dew in the light. A simple fence cordoned us off from entering further, and the entrance wasn't to open for another couple of hours, so having taken in as much as we could, we jogged home.

\*     \*     \*     \*

We scoffed down breakfast, eager to explore the city. Samarkand had been occupied for so long, and for a moment in time by such an earth-shaking empire, that it was simply littered with history. And while the Registan was perhaps its most famous structure, it was the Gur-e-Amir that we chose to head to first, Tamerlane's tomb.

\*     \*     \*     \*

The Gur-e-Amir or "Tomb of the King" was actually constructed by Tamerlane in 1403 as a Mausoleum for his favourite grandchild after he'd died on his return from defeating the Ottoman Empire. But when Tamerlane died two years later, he was interred here as were eventually his sons and later grandchildren including Ulugh Beg—the 'astronomer-King', arguably the last worthy leader of his empire before it collapsed.

We paid our small entrance fee and entered through a hallway that led to the tomb. Green onyx tiles with white marble Koranic inscriptions lined the walls before opening up into the tomb itself, the ceiling presenting an infinite amount of detail in blue and gold that glittered in the light from a hanging chandelier. The complicated geometric patterns were made up of Girih tiles, a specialised architectural feature of Islamic art where intricate interlinked patterns are formed using five specific shaped tiles. Together these tiles form extremely mathematically complex shapes. So complex that they were independently 'theorised' in the 1970s by an American physicist who proposed these shapes as a way of constructing impossible crystal structures[*]. It has been suggested that the complexity in Islamic art is a consequence of the prohibition on depicting animal and human form, forcing artistic talent to find new ways to express itself.

On the floor of the chamber sat the marble tombstone slabs of each of Tamerlane's descendants and a large dark green jade slab for Tamerlane himself. It was said that this slab—the largest slab of Jade in the world at the time—had

---

[*]   See the book *Second Kind of Impossible*.

been taken from a Chinese Emperor's Palace by the Mongols almost two centuries prior to Tamerlane, and had been transported here via a specially constructed vehicle. Inscribed onto the slab was written "When I rise from the dead, the world will tremble". And it is said that on the inside of the slab is written "Whoever so disturbs my tomb will unleash an invader more terrible than I". Well it turned out that the invader was Hitler, for when a Soviet archaeologist—so the myth goes—opened the slab in search of Tamerlane's remains in 1941, it was announced two hours later that Nazi Germany had declared war on Soviet Russia. After much consternation, his body was reinterred with full Muslim rights in 1942, with the Nazi's surrendering at Stalingrad only a short while later. Implying a rather petty God, who was also presumably Russian. What the archaeologist found though was that yes—Tamerlane (Timur the Lame) was in fact lame in his right leg and arm, and stood at roughly 170 cm. A cm taller than Napoleon.

We wandered back out, just as a tour bus pulled up to deposit a group of white-haired old ladies who were gently stepping down and off to pay their respects to the evilest man in the world.

Adjacent to his Mausoleum sat another, the Rukhobod Mausoleum which like the Khoja Ahmed Yasawi Mausoleum we had seen in Turkestan. It too had been built by Tamerlane as a sign of respect to an Islamic scholar reminding people that despite his cruelty, he was also pious. Despite the millions of mainly Muslims he killed, he was also "the shadow of God on Earth".

We exited the park through two impressive lion 'guardian' statues, and headed up towards the Registan. It was late morning by now and to our shock, a (very) few tourists had started coalescing around the entrance and another 10 or 15 were wandering around the Registan square, all dwarfed by the structures at their sides. Paying our minimal entrance fee, we soon joined the other tourists and became part of the spectacle. The portals* of each madrassah loomed over us, along with their columns, some of which had taken on a lean with age. Splashes of colour filled out the geometric patterns gracing the surfaces, while Koranic verses written in mixtures of stones ran across various surfaces. Each element of each madrassah was filled with entirely different patterns and colours that altogether was complimentary rather than clashing. The perhaps one unusual element of it all was the Sher-Dor Madrassah which featured both a large swastika above its entrance, and two flame orange tigers carrying what seemed to be the faces of people. It was interesting to consider that the Islamic prohibition on the depiction of animals and people was so conspicuously being flounced here. That these Indian looking design elements were built at a time when the Indian Mughal Empire were reengaging with their Uzbek neighbours, may have had something to do with it. On the other side of each madrassah's portals

---

\*    The front facing entrance to a Madrassah or Mosque.

were large courtyards, their perimeter lined with cover that served as workshops to various artisans. The spectacle of the Registan was striking. Details so delicate, colours so brilliant, and scales so impressive, for the modern traveller it was simply astounding. For the ancient traveller on the other hand, many of whom would've arrived after a perilous and destitute journey through the deserts of modern Turkmenistan, this must've appeared almost unworldly. Just the impression I suppose that they were meant to convey.

We left the Registan and carried on along the manicured Tashkent Road, perfectly tiled and lined with trimmed hedges, a road that was often pointed to as an example of the 'Disneyfication' of Samarkand. Unlike Bukhara and Khiva, which had been left more alone, Samarkand was a polished version of itself, something that many criticised. But *so what* I thought, these buildings were astounding, and the grounds amongst them should reflect that. If those critics wanted more authenticity, then I point them to the paintings of the 19th century, where substituting for neatly trimmed hedges were rows of Russian heads upon spikes. And if many of these buildings hadn't been restored, then a lot of what we were looking at would simply be ruins. Such as the Bibi-Khanym Mosque built by Tamerlane following his conquests of India, wrecked by an earthquake in the 19th century before it was restored by the Ubzeki government in the 1970s. And had it not been restored, we wouldn't have been able to walk through its entrance, sparkling blue in the sun, and into its beautiful courtyard with its neatly trimmed lawn shaded by pretty trees.

Ubzeki artisans sat around the edge of this courtyard, selling woodwork and carpets to the one or two other tourists milling about. I wandered over to one of the stalls just as the craftsman added the final touch to a delicately carved wooden panel before lightly blowing it, holding it up to inspect it, and then satisfied at what must've been a laborious process, placed it amongst the others. I politely lifted it up, aware of the craftsmanship I'd just witnessed, and studied it. Such extraordinary detail I remarked before handing over the requested small fortune. I suppose I should've realised that it was highly unlikely that he'd have finished the piece the moment I walked over, but as yet hadn't read of the factories nearby banging these out by the thousand.

Either way, it was one more specimen to add to my growing pile of Central Asian tourist trinkets, and noting that my bag was at capacity, determined that I better offload some of these things to the world.

*   *   *   *

Having originally envisioned myself cruising through deserts on land cruisers, potentially wearing aviators, I had imagined that trudging a suitcase around would've been both impractical and uncool. So I instead opted for a duffel bag. But given the need for clothing for the snow *and* the desert, the cities *and* the mountains, the bag had since landing in Almaty been stretching at the seams and slowly forming a divot between my neck and shoulder. Meaning I was sensitive to any unnecessary weight. Each morning I would

**ANGISTAU, KAZAHKSTAN** My friend deep in contemplation and confusion of where he is.

**BUKHARA** Looking out from the Kalan Mosque

▲ **A ONCE MIGHTY CITADEL** in the ancient city of Merv

▲ **LOOKING DOWN UPON THE MOUNTAIN RANGES** that separate
Kazahkstan from Kyrgystan and China

▲ **SLAVES IN BUKHARA** turn of the 20th century

▲ **GETTING LOST IN THE DESERTS OF KAZAHKSTAN** with nothing in sight but for the wild horses that once made Genghis Khan so violently succesful.

▲ **THOUSANDS OF METRES ABOVE SEA LEVEL,** in the Ala Archa park above Bishkek, capital of Kyrgyztan

▲ **LATE 19TH CENTURY PAINTING** depicting Samarkand with the heads of Russian soliders on stakes

▲ **CHARYON CANYON**, Kazahkstan's answer to the Grand Canyon

▲ **THE LAST EMIR OF BUKHARA** deposed by the Bolsheviks in the 1920's

▲ **RECONSTRUCTION OF TAMERLANE** based on his skull

▲ **LOOKING OUT ACROSS KHIVA** in the late afternoon

▲ **INTERIOR OF THE MAUSOLEUM** to the conqueror king and worst human in history, Tamerlane

▲ **THE ENORMOUS AND UNFINISHED MAUSOLEUM** to a Sufi Preacher, commissioned by Tamerlane in teh 14th century

▲ **GETTING READY FOR A HOME COOKED MEAL** in the mountains of Kyrgystan

▲ **A YOUNG KAZAKH COUPLE** having their marriage photos taken, before requesting a blessing from me – the foreigner

▲ **OLD SOVIET RADAR STATION** on the border of Uzbekistan and Kyrgystan

▲ **THE HOLIDAY RESIDENCE OF TURKMENISTAN'S DICTATOR,** amongst the mountains above Dushanbe

▲ **KYRGYZTAN MOUNTAIN RANGES** looking decidedly Swiss, or perhaps its the other way around

▲ **THE KYZ KALA OR 'MAIDENS CASTLE'** where 40 virgins threw themselves to their death rather than face the Mongols streaming below during their destruction of Merv, Turkmenistan

▲ **THE OUTER CITY WALLS** of Khiva, Uzbekistan

▲ **LAKE ISKANDERKUL,** high up in the mountains above Dushanbe, capital of Tajikistan. Named after Alexander the Great who passed by here on his way into India.

▲ **THE KALYAN MINARET,** or 'Tower of Death' being seranaded with the theme of Star Wars

▲ **INTERIOR OF THE ARK** (citadel) sitting inside the walls of Khiva, Uzbekistan

▲ **THE BUKHARAN 'ARK'** where British Captains Stoddart and Connolly were held for years before being beheaded on the courtyard

▲ **AN 18TH CENTURY MOSQUE** in Khiva, Uzbekistan

▲ **GOAT HERDERS** in the countryside of Tajikistan

▲ **SAMARKAND,** the 'Taj Mahal' of Central Asia.

▲ **MY DRIVER IN OSH,** Kyrgyzstan who turned out to be only a few years older than me

▲ **THE REMANANTS** of the extremely hot petroleum wax applied to my downstairs
operation as part of an old Soviet health treatment in Tajikistan

▲ **LOOKING DOWN AT BIZARRO LAND** that is Ashgabat, capital of Turkmenistan

▲ **RUSSIAN TROOPS ENTERING,** and eventually capturing, the city of Khiva.

▲ **THE FINAL HUNT OF THE DAY** Capturing 500 Kazahk tenge from an Austra

▲ **MANGISTAU, KAZAHKSTAN** The outer edge of the salt fla

knock back a multivitamin and feel inwardly satisfied that I'd made my bag lighter. And when I found an old boarding pass at the bottom of my bag, I kicked myself thinking I'd been lugging around such a useless piece of weight. What it also meant was that I was always eager to offload the steadily accumulating gifts (primarily to myself) and so decided that I would whisk off to a Samarkand post office and send forth my gifts to their respective giftees (primarily myself).

Weaving through backstreets, I arrived at the post office, a large derelict hall filled with a lingering smell of burning wood. I approached a counter, pointed at my items and with my hand made the image of a plane taking off, holding myself back from instinctively coupling it with aeroplane noises. The lady behind the counter got my drift and pointed to her colleague. I shifted to her colleague and through extreme gesticulation, I made it clear that I wanted these items sent to Australia, New Zealand and the USA. The lady handed me some forms while I flashed her my credit card and nodded to ask whether I could use it. No, shook the lady's head. Shit, I thought, as I had no Uzbeki Som, yet after some explanation including the lady behind the counter mimicking the use of an ATM, I determined that there existed a bank a mere 15 minutes' walk away. I left my items with the lady who had been inspecting them, indicating that I would be back, and sprinted off to the bank.

There were two ATMs at the bank, one which didn't accept my card, the other only giving USD. A lovely old lady behind an information desk suggested in broken English that I withdraw USD and exchange it over there, pointing to a long queue that led to a booth. I placed myself in the stationary queue and could immediately sense a growing agitation amongst the men in front of me, one of whom eventually placed his head through the booth and began wildly gesticulating and yelling at the staff. It didn't seem to have an effect other than to make everyone else in the queue start yelling too. It quickly became apparent that the bank had run out or at least was unwilling to give out Uzbeki Som only heightening the agitation of the room. Not speaking Ubzek, I sadly couldn't partake in the yelling but was saved when a young woman, wearing not only the first tattoo I'd seen in the country but was covered from head to toe, suggested to me to follow her to another bank.

We hastily left the bank and darted across to another where I handed over my USD$200. Being the equivalent of 1,660,000 Uzbeki Som, I was given a *Weimer Republic* looking amount of money which I duly stuffed into my bulging pockets.

I rushed back to the post office where my gifts were in the final stages of being processed. Each item was wrapped in layers of scrap cloth with the international addresses written awkwardly with a marker, before a stick pulled from a bucket of hot wax was used to wax seal it altogether. Rope was produced, tying each package up into irregular football-shaped parcels, before they were placed in a large bin. Satisfied with her work, the lady took out a form written in Cyrillic, scribbled a tracking number on it and handed it over. Well, it was the thought that counted I thought to myself never expecting to see those items again. That I and my friends did, surely must say something about the sophistication of the global postal system.

*     *     *     *

For our final evening, we made our way to Platan Restaurant, the number 2 restaurant on TripAdvisor, to join every other tourist in the city (roughly 15) who had read the same memo. Sadly, the memo hadn't been read by the staff, who acted overwhelmed by the more than one customer, indifferently taking our orders and extending out our dinner as if the restaurant was only *acting* as a profit-driven enterprise. Which surely must've been what dining out had been like during the Soviet Union, remarked Andrew. Finishing the journey that was our dinner, we hailed down the first car that we saw and shot back off to the Registan which we had read was splendidly lit up each night.

We arrived moments later, stepping out into the balmy air, and onto the platform in front of the Registan. Golden floodlights bathed the structure, gloriously catching the polished tiles and causing each madrassah to glow. Perhaps it was the wine, but wandering amongst the glittering jewellery box of a structure, on a still evening under a sky filled with stars, I couldn't help but think 'only 5% of the world's population huh…'

# BUKHARA

I t was early afternoon as we arrived to the open-air platform of the Bukhara train station. The sun sat still in the
cloudless blue sky as we and the other passengers disem-
barked onto the platform, taking a moment to stretch. The
loud whirring of the train's engine which for the past hour
and a half had simply become background noise disappeared
as the engines were cut, draping us in a sudden stillness. All
of which served to heighten the abruptness of exiting the
quiet train station and entering the tumultuous scrum of
Uzbeks crowding around its entrance all vying for this new
set of arrivals. Being the few non-Uzbeks made us particularly lucrative targets and meant we had to hustle our way
through the first few layers of people before making it out
into the relative open. Three Uzbeks flashing their gold tooth
smiles followed us as we walked to the station's car park,

each throwing out a price to take us into town. Finding this process particularly uncomfortable, I left it to Andrew who after a short amount of haggling chose the bloke with the least teeth, who then beckoned us over to his beaten-up car and shot us off onto the motorway.

The train station sat at the outskirts of the city and we were now racing down the motorway that took us through these outer parts made up of cheap cookie-cutter housing developments, and the occasional big block retailer sitting alone in a field. All the consequences of a poor modern society which abruptly changed into that of a rich ancient one as the cheaply built apartments made way for tightly packed sand coloured housing and brightly decorated mosques. With only a handful of streets in ancient Bukhara able to handle cars, our driver could only take us so far and deposited us at the entrance to the Toqi Telpak Furushon, a 16th century bazaar whose tall pointed arches had once welcomed caravans travelling the Silk Road. Thankfully, I had the previous day offloaded several heavy items into the ether of the Uzbekistan postal service, so only had a slight hobble to my walk as Andrew and I searched for our hotel.

*   *   *   *

The city had been founded two and a half thousand years ago by the Zoroastrian Persian Empire, and was visited by Alexander and his army almost two centuries later after having brought that empire to its knees. Being situated on the Zeravshan River, the same river that upstream ran through

Samarkand, Bukhara was an oasis in the centre of an otherwise dry desert landscape that attracted the caravans working the early Silk Road. This, in turn, led to an accumulation of wealth and infrastructure, inadvertently placing a target on itself for future invaders. The first were the Arab armies who turned up to the city in 673AD. Unlike later outsiders, they were happy to leave the city and its people intact so long as they paid their tribute and adopted Islam. To the average Bukharan this meant renouncing their Nestorian Christian faith, a sect of Christianity that had been establishing itself across Central Asia since the mid-400s*.

Initially, the city adopted an only outwardly Islamic appearance, but by the 9th century, it had become fully entrenched and indeed began to flourish. Madrassas and mosques were built at a rapid pace, attracting Muslim scholars from across the Islamic world, only increasing the need for more Islamic institutions. By the medieval period, Bukhara had become a global hot spot for the Islamic faith and began being referred to as 'The Dome of Islam in the East'. It was regarded as being so holy that it was often said—presumably by people who had never been there—that light shone upwards from the city, illuminating heaven.

As the new millennium came about, the Arabs who had swept into the region started getting swept out and replaced

---

* It was due to these Arab armies, that Christianity fell to the wayside in Central Asia and which by the 14th century was largely wiped out leaving only pockets remaining in India.

as new groups of Persians and Turkic tribes took their place. By the 13<sup>th</sup> century, Bukhara had become part of the Khwarazmian Dynasty. And it was at this stage that the city exploded in size and importance, becoming home to over 300,000 people, rivalling Baghdad—then perhaps the most important city in the world—in both artistic and scholarly output and in trade. Sadly, however, this was also the century of the Mongols, and when the ruler of the Khwarazmian Dynasty—Shah Ala Muhammad—made what perhaps must be one of history's great historic blunders.

$$*\quad*\quad*\quad*$$

While Genghis Khan had been successfully battling the Chinese to the Empire's north, he had sent an envoy to the Shah to establish trade routes between the two nations. Having received reports of Mongol savagery, the governor who received the envoy ordered most of the envoy beheaded and the remainder disfigured and sent back. Furious, Genghis demanded that the governor be handed over to him and a tribute be paid as reparations, but the Shah refused. In response, Genghis Khan rerouted his army south and into the Khwarazmian Empire, marching first on the city of Otras in modern Kazakhstan, home of the offending governor.

It took five months of siege warfare against Otras before Genghis was able to sweep across it. The governor who was holed up in the city's citadel fought right to the end, reportedly throwing tiles down on the Mongols below him, killing some in the process. Eventually, though he was caught alive and brought before Genghis Khan who had him executed by pouring molten silver into his eyes and throat. With transgression number one rectified, Genghis next turned towards rectifying transgression number two, which meant finding and executing the Shah who had rejected his demands. The Shah, aware of his impending doom, headed south and holed himself up with a garrison of soldiers, in the city of Bukhara.

Genghis and his army of 70,000 arrived at Bukhara in early 1220, which at the time was being defended by the Shah's garrison of 20,000. Upon seeing the Mongol army in the distance, much of this garrison, along with the Shah himself packed up and fled into the desert, leaving the city largely undefended. When Genghis arrived at the gates, he entered Bukhara unopposed and marched directly to the central mosque while ordering the rounding up of the population. He demanded that the 280 wealthiest and most eminent of the population be brought to him and in a scene captured in a painting, painted 200 years later, took the podium and made the following speech:

*O people, know that you have committed great sins, and that the great ones among you have committed these sins. If you ask me what proof I have for these words, I say it is because I am the punishment of God. If you had not committed great sin, God would not have sent a punishment like me upon you.*

He stepped down from the mosque while the 280 people were marched off to reveal their and the city's stores of wealth and led his army to the citadel where a few remaining loyal soldiers to the Shah had barricaded themselves.

Today named the Ark Fortress, the citadel that Genghis Khan arrived at 800 years ago, sits solidly in the centre of the city and is used as a staging point for festivals and formal events. Built up with bricks sitting on earthen mounds, its walls form big pregnant bellies of structure that push outward, their crenelated tops sitting 20 m above the ground. A large ramp enters up through its single central entrance, the entrance flanked by two guard towers and a defensive structure on top. It was already 1200 years old by the time Genghis arrived, and the successive rulers of the city over the previous thousand and so years had each added to it, making it more formidable with every addition. From the ground level today, it seems almost impenetrable, too steep and high to easily climb and too solid to destroy. For Genghis though, who on the back of successful campaigns against the Chinese had mastered the art of siege warfare, this meant little.

Initially, however, rather than wasting the lives of his soldiers on what was a well-defended and equipped citadel, Genghis decided he would waste those of the newly captured citizens and marched them against the Ark. The soldiers inside had no choice but to defend themselves and launched flaming oil against their Bukharan brethren. After launching waves of Bukharan citizens against the Ark over the course of a week, Genghis next opened with his Chinese captured siege weapons. These included trebuchets, catapults and crossbow-like machines that could launch arrows the size of small telegraph poles. The defence of the citadel was soon overwhelmed with the remaining defending soldiers, according to a Persian eyewitness, "drowning in the sea of annihilation".* Genghis had captured and defeated the city of Bukhara. He had most of its population murdered but for the artisans and craftsmen who would help build his Mongol cities in the north, women who would become sex slaves to his army, but all of whom would live lives of servitude until their deaths.

With this captured population under the control of his army, he left the city and marched on to Samarkand, but not before setting fire to the city and razing *almost* all of it to the ground. The Ark, however, avoided destruction and over the next few centuries would become again the citadel to the new rulers of the city, and the prison to many others. Amongst those prisoners, almost 600 years after Genghis had left, were two young British spies who in the Great Game between the British and Russian Empires, had found themselves imprisoned there.

*    *    *    *

Charles Stoddart had been a British diplomat, spy and adventurer operating out of British India, who in 1838 had been dispatched by the British East India Company to meet

---

\* *Genghis Khan and the Making of the New World,* Jack Weatherford.

with the Emir of Bukhara, Nasrullah Khan. By this stage Genghis Khan had come and gone, Tamerlane had long since died, Bukhara had rebuilt itself from the ashes and the region had settled into an uneasy truce between three Khanates, the Khanate of Bukhara being but one. To the south of Bukhara lay Afghanistan which at the time was being meddled with by the Russians, an action that Britain saw as the initial steps towards a full invasion of British India. Intending to forestall this, in 1839 the British invaded Afghanistan ostensibly to install the "rightful" ruler to the country, in what became known as the First Anglo-Afghan War. Four thousand five hundred British troops became stationed in Kabul along with 12,000 civilians which along with craftsmen, tailors, barbers, armourers, etc. included the families of the soldiers. To ensure to the Emir of Bukhara that this occupying force to his south posed no threat to his rule, and to secure an allegiance between him and the British Empire, the British sent Stoddart to negotiate with him.

The Emir of Bukhara was not some simple benevolent ruler though. He had come to power by murdering all of his brothers, along with another 28 other relatives, treated his population savagely and sadistically, held the nickname 'The Butcher' and who, rumour had it, had once personally chopped one of his military generals in half with an axe. So when Stoddart arrived and rather than following Bukharan etiquette of dismounting from his horse—walking on foot through the city gates and bowing before the Emir, instead followed British Cavalry protocol of trotting in on his horse and saluting from his saddle—the Emir was not happy. And after failing to present any gifts from the British Monarch who the Emir saw as his equal, and then proceeding to commit a series of minor gaffes, ever confident in his position as a representative of Imperial Britain, the Emir flew into a rage and threw Stoddart into 'the pit'. This pit, infamously known as the 'bug-pit' was purposefully filled with vermin and rats that the guards would feed with offal, and was situated deep inside the Ark. "I don't understand where he was meant to crap", I exclaimed to the guide who along with myself and Andrew were peering down deep into this pit. "In the corner", was the reply. Having been lowered down by rope, Stoddart languished there for two years anxiously waiting for either his rescue or his execution. His treatment was not consistent, however, and as the fortunes of the British in the region rose and fell, so did his treatment when at one-point Stoddart was shifted from the bug-pit to simple house arrest. It was during this moment that Stoddart was able to smuggle a note out which made its way back to British India and into the hands of the British Indian Governor-General.

Arthur Connelly had been the quintessential player of the Great Game. Youthful, adventurous and supremely confident in himself and in British superiority. He had been in the region for years and had been covertly exploring on behalf of the British East India Company under the pseudonym of 'Khan Ali', a play on his last name. When the note arrived at the British India headquarters, it was Connelly, aged 33, that the British Indian Governor-General sent to save Stoddart. In disguise as a travelling pilgrim, he arrived at Bukhara in November 1841 and was able to freely explore the city, even meeting with Stoddart who he was shocked to discover emaciated and covered in sores. Unfortunately, while Connelly was roaming around the city, the Emir received a letter from Dost Mohammed, the Afghan leader who had been disposed by the British, outing this 'Khan Ali' as a British spy. In a rage, the Emir had Connelly arrested and along with Stoddart thrown back in the pit. In the meantime, back in Afghanistan that same Dost Mohmmad was leading a successful uprising against the British occupiers, forcing the British into negotiating their retreat. The terms of the retreat were onerous, including handing over their gunpowder reserves, their newest muskets and most of their canons. In exchange, however, the sick and infirm British that had to remain were to be looked after, and the 4,500 soldiers and 12,000 men, women and children civilians were guaranteed a safe passage out of the city and all the way to the British garrison in Jalalabad. Yet almost immediately after the retreat had begun, Dost Mahammad's army swept in setting fire to the British cantonments, killing those British sick and wounded left behind, and began firing on the retreating soldiers. The picking off the backline of the British retreat soon devolved into an ambush which by the third day had killed 3,000 of the British force, by the sixth 12,000 and by the seventh all of them. All except for one, an assistant surgeon who stumbled into Jalalabad on a pony and who when asked what had happened to the army reportedly answered 'I am the army'.

When news of this arrived in Bukhara, the fates of Connelly and Stoddart were sealed. With their hair and beards crawling with lice, they were dragged out from the bug-pit and marched to the square in front of the Ark where a crowd along with the Emir had gathered. After being forced to kneel in front of the graves they had just dug, the Emir gave the signal to the executioner who swung down with his sword first beheading Stoddart and then Connelly. And so, Stoddart and Connelly, the by all account brave British subjects, ended their lives brutally in a hostile foreign land, thousands of kilometres away from home at the ages of 33 and 34 respectively, the same age as I was while standing there in Bukhara. The British writer Colin Thubron had passed through this city in the early 2000s and had found a local who knew where they had been buried. Supposedly on the edge of the city in a lonely spot under a tree. "Do you know where they are buried?" I asked the manager of the hotel we were staying at. "No, I don't, but it was only Stoddart that was beheaded, Connelly was released", came the incorrect reply.

*   *   *   *

It was lunchtime by the time Andrew and I had finished at the Ark, and based on the recommendation of our hotel manager, continued walking to the farmer's market where we were told the locals did their shopping.

Beggars surrounded the entrance of the market as thousands of people swarmed amongst the vendors, themselves screaming from their stalls. Smoke from roasting nuts mixed with the smell of stacked samosas and the raw meat hanging from the stalls, all intensified by the heat of the day. A man approached us and angrily shouted at us before someone pushed him away. I pushed my money deeper into my pockets. We worked our way through the stalls and the people, out from the food section and into the endless rows of second-hand clothing and consumer goods. A travelling Hungarian Armin Vambery who had passed through here 170 years before us had remarked that he'd seen goods marked 'Manchester' and 'Birmingham', though noting the Cantonese characters, it was China that dominated these markets today. With so much *stuff* everywhere, it was hard to understand how anyone was making any money.

Amongst the piles of cheap Chinese appliances and clothing, we found a tiny restaurant and sat down at the white plastic table and chairs at its entrance. It was impossible to determine the menu, so we asked for whatever the waitress suggested to which she returned with two plates of greasy meat in a watery sauce. With some apprehension, we finished our meal, handing our plates back to the waitress who placed them onto a pile of used dishes in a dirty sink. But for the general spectacle, the market didn't offer us anything, and suspecting we'd soon be in need of a bathroom, we left.

The remnants of an ancient city wall bumped up against the market, which we were able to get through via the impressive

Talipach Gate, once the entrance for caravans arriving to the city from the North. Behind was a green and leafy park, offering some respite from the bustle of the marketplace. And amongst the trees sat a lonely Mausoleum, built around 900 AD which was said to make it the oldest known monument of Islamic architecture in Central Asia. A flood had buried it under mud two centuries after it was built, ironically saving it by hiding it from Genghis and his army who arrived soon after. In fact, it was only rediscovered in the early 20$^{th}$ century after two years of excavation by Soviet archaeologists. It had been built as a mausoleum to Ismail Samani, the ruler of the Samanid Empire, a Sunni Islamic Empire that had ruled over parts of modern Central Asia and Afghanistan. Interestingly, I was to see a towering statue of Samani weeks later in Dushanbe, the capital of Tajikistan, where the Tajiks hold him to be the father of the Tajiks. Indeed, he is held in such high esteem there that they renamed what had been the tallest mountain in the Soviet Union at 7,495 m, from Communism Peak to Samoni Peak. His face appears on what had been the largest banknote (until inflation forced the creation of a couple more), and moreover, his name *is* the currency—the Tajikistani Samoni. All of which serves as an interesting illustration of the changing demographics of the region, where the resting place for the father of the Tajiks sits in the land of the Uzbeks. We left this Mausoleum and continued through the park, walking out and back past the Ark again before carrying on towards perhaps the most prominent landmark in the city, the Kalyan Minaret.

*    *    *    *

The Kalyan Minaret had been built in 1127, during the Kara-Khanid Khanate that had ruled the region after sweeping away the Samanid Empire—the empire that had been ruled by the Tajik's founder. Reaching 46 m into the sky, and another 10 m underground it was at the time of its completion one of the tallest minarets in the world and had so impressed Genghis Khan when he arrived, that seemingly out of character, he spared it from destruction. Less than a century later an unknown Italian architect passed through the city and shared the Great Khan's opinion of it, going on to copy the geometric patterns onto the Doge's Palace in Venice, built in 1340. The Bolsheviks took a slightly dimmer view, and after arriving in the early 20th century had a go at its destruction with a bombing campaign that levelled parts of the city and tore chunks from the tower. But it still stood and in the late 90s was repaired and refurbished. Its name simply means 'Big Tower' but for a long time it was referred to as the 'Tower of Death'. Not because its foundations contain the head of a murdered imam, but owing to the grisly fact that for many centuries, and even for a few years into the 20th, criminals were led to the top, tied up in bags to contain the mess and thrown off. On either side of it sat the Mir-i-Arab Madrassa and the Kalan Mosque, connected to the minaret by a small bridge. And amongst all of this, across the plaza that sat at the centre, were groups of sound technicians testing the acoustics of large speakers.

I tried asking one of the workers what was happening, but he spoke no English and showed very little enthusiasm in talking to me, so I gave up.

We walked across to the entrance of the Kalan Mosque where an old, leathery skinned Uzbeki man was sitting selling antique watches, one of which caught Andrew's eye. I left him there to barter as I entered the mosque.

It had been built on the destroyed foundations of a previous Mosque that Genghis Khan had razed, making it *only* 500 years old. It was beautiful and made up of an inner courtyard, with a fountain at one end, and 208 pillars holding up the 288 domes that served as its perimeter. From the hot and dusty bustle of the plaza outside, its interior offered a cool and quiet reprieve. Small groups of conservatively dressed women shuffled amongst the pillars, while a foreign couple quietly wandered around the courtyard taking photos. With the sun low on the horizon, I was able to snap beautiful shots of the large Mihrab* that stood at one end blocking the sun, but glowing blue as the sun shone around its edges catching it's multitude of Azul tiles. I walked back towards the semi-circle entrance, which framed the opposite madrassah covered in tiles, and a turquoise dome beaming back and beautifully reflecting the sun. Andrew was still haggling. He'd picked up a retro watch with the Uzbekistan flag, some writing in Cyrillic and '1943 to 1993' on its face.

---

* The mihrab being a feature of Islamic architecture that indicates the direction of Mecca.

"The guy won't budge, he's trying to rip me off", my exasperated friend said.

"What does he want for it?"

"Sixteen bucks",

"And what are you offering",

"Fifteen".

"For Christ's sake, it's a single dollar". Andrew pondered for a bit, nodded in resignation, and begrudgingly shook the hand of the seller. The seller muttered something in Uzbek and threw his hands up into the air, as if to say *finally*. They shook hands, and as the money was exchanged, the seller pointed out "When it stops working each day, pull this out and give it a wind".

\*    \*    \*    \*

We returned to the plaza and the minaret later that night after learning that the speakers were being set up for a concert. What had been empty but for a smattering of tourists and the occasional unfriendly sound technician, had now evolved into what seemed like the entire town filling rows of chairs, with large groups of people piling up behind them. Police officers conspicuously meandered around while a conductor standing in front of a full piece orchestra[*] spoke to the crowd through a microphone. The minaret was lit up from its base in a bright purple hue, the light pulling out the details of the complex brickwork through their shadows.

---

[*]    It turned out to be the National Symphony Orchestra of Uzbekistan

The conductor stopped talking, bowed to the audience, and turned to face his orchestra. As the crowd hushed itself into silence, the conductor lifted his hands above his head and held them for a moment before dropping them and launching into the theme song for Star Wars. Which took Andrew and I by complete surprise, though it dawned on me that this was rather fitting given the desert, sand and medieval-style world that much of that film was set in. We watched and listened to this and the next song—the theme to Jaws—before retreating into the alleyways of Bukhara in search of dinner.

We peered around the corner and through a large arched doorway which opened into the courtyard of some visibly ancient buildings. At its centre was an old tree hanging over a charming pond, trickling water along open conduits that ran under the tables and chairs of a quiet restaurant. We walked in and took a seat as an Uzbeki man followed us, sitting down adjacent to us before placing his phone on the table and pressing play on a video with the volume turned up to its maximum. Like an old married couple, Andrew and I argued under our breath, with him insisting that I shouldn't say anything. To be fair to him, this man looked thuggish and probably wouldn't like being told to turn his phone down by two skinny foreigners. I inconspicuously motioned for the waiter who approached as if in cahoots. Digging deep into my British heritage, I quietly asked while simultaneously apologising to the waiter "Could you please, if it's alright, ask the man next to us, please, to turn his phone down, thank you". She closed her eyes and nodded in quiet under-standing, lifted her head and yelled in Ubzeki at the top of her voice at the man, before disappearing into the kitchen.

\*     \*     \*     \*

The following day was the final morning for Andrew and I as he was leaving early on a train the next day to Samarkand, and then onto Almaty for his return flight home. We de-cided to spend part of the day visiting what had been the summer palace of the Emir of Bukhara sitting on the out-skirts of the city and rented a couple of bikes to get us there. Unfortunately for us, what looked like a reasonably straight-forward route from our hotel to the Palace turned out to be a major arterial road four lanes wide, being treated by Uzbeki drivers as if they were eight. Attempting to stick to the pave-ment proved futile as the lack of suspension, broken concrete pavement and small hardened bike seats conspired to turn our bikes into a contraption out of *120 Days of Sodom*. After fighting our way through the obstacle course that is Uzbeki infrastructure and narrowly avoiding being hit by a couple of cars, we eventually arrived at the Sitorai Mohi-Hosa Palace.

The name meant 'the stars and the moon of the Emir' and had been built for the last governing Emir by the Russian Empire who was more than happy to have the Emir stationed outside of the city, rather than in it along with his garrison and obedient mullahs. Constructed over two decades at the turn of the 20th century, it was designed by both Russian and Uzbeki architects who together fused an odd mix of medieval

Central Asian Islamic architect with the grandness of a royal residence in St. Petersburg. An interesting by-product of two very different worlds colliding. This wasn't, however, the Emir's primary Palace, but rather a summer 'pleasure palace' with an emphasis on the pleasure. Entering through the grand archway, covered in mosaic tiles, and into one of the two courtyards, sidestepping the tamed peacocks and then walking through the 'Hall of Mirrors' and into the throne room, a visiting dignitary may not have fully appreciated that. But had they carried on and into the second courtyard, they would have come across the large multi-story building that was home to 400 women and 40 'dancing boys' that made up the Emir's harem. And perhaps may have seen some of that harem frolicking in the purposefully constructed adjacent pond, with the Emir overlooking them all from his elaborately decorated raised pavilion. It was said that the Emir would sit here and throw an apple to one of his harem who he would then have washed in donkey's milk and delivered to his bedroom. Sadly for the Emir, that bastion of Islam in Central Asia, his harem was released when the Bolsheviks arrived in September of 1920, freeing them along with issuing a proclamation "declaring that the Emir's wives were now divorced from him and were free to leave and marry whom they wished".* Though by this point, what may have been at fore and front of the Emir's mind was regaining his empire which the Bolsheviks had just captured.

---

\* Taken verbatim from Peter Hopkirk's Setting the East Ablaze

This, however, was no abrupt surprise attack on the Emir's empire, as for the previous two years he had been suffering under the growing threat of an internal Soviet revolution by young Bukharans. And despite how much sadistic torture he had his soldiers inflict on the revolutionaries he caught; the ideology of communism proved to be more appealing than the savage society he imposed on his people. After realising that he could no longer stem this revolutionary tide, he prepared to leave along with his enormous wealth, which included thirty-five million pounds sterling in gold and silver coins and ingots. To transfer this wealth out of the city without it being captured, he appealed to the British agents that had been clandestinely operating in the city since the Russian Empire had been overthrown. "To secure the safety of his wealth", reported Lieutenant-Colonel Etherton, "he offered to confide it to our care, and requested us to take charge of it pending the dawn of bright days and a return to normal conditions". The physical mechanics behind moving such a large amount of treasure from such an isolated city proved, however, to be insurmountable. The Emir was forced to flee his city, which he did *just* as the Bolsheviks arrived, escaping with his frightened followers to the neighbouring town of Denau. Here he sat for four days; a period best described by Joshua Kunitz in his 1936 book *Dawn over Samarkand:*

> *The first day, peasants by the thousands milled around the house where the Emir was lodged, anxious to get at least one glimpse at the divine being they so often blessed in their*

*Friday prayers. By the end of the second day however, there
was not a peasant left in Denau. They had all sought refuge
in the villages, hiding their young wives and daughters,
smearing dung over the faces of the prettiest youngsters.*

The Emir couldn't stay here though, as the Red Army
had turned east in their hunt for him, forcing him first to
Dushanbe, and then to Kabul where he remained until his
death in 1944.

\*     \*     \*     \*

It was the final night Andrew and I had together and on any
normal occasion, we would've gone for at least a drink. On
this instance though, we were both struck by food poisoning
and could hardly muster up the energy to even get to dinner.
We did though, and tired and wary scoffed down a couple of
Russian Borsches, before wandering back to our hotel, where
I fell into a deep sleep. I had emails to respond to, books to
read, and felt like spending some time in a gym all in order
to reset the body for the next leg of my trip. And so, when
I woke up the next morning—Andrew now gone—I wandered out for a light breakfast before making my way to a
gym I'd found on Google.

\*     \*     \*     \*

I rented a bicycle from outside my hotel and rode the way
there, initially through the ancient backstreets and then onto
an outer main road. I was recovering from a third bout of

food poisoning in almost as few weeks, so was tired and irritable which didn't make things easier as my decrepit old bike struggled against the potholed roads. I rode past a group of Uzbeks who simply stared back with a conspicuous lack of agreeableness. A car drove up behind me and gave a sharp whack of his horn. "These bloody Uzbeks", I shouted to myself as the shoddy old Mercedes spluttered off past me. I finally found what I thought to be the gym and climbed the steps down into a seedy dark windowless basement with various doors around the perimeter. At one end was a grubby counter, and a nasty looking kid sitting on a highchair. "Gym?" I said to the kid while mimicking the lifting of weights. He scrunched his face up at me in scorn. I looked around at the closed doors, muffled noises and strips of light coming from the gaps between the floor and their bases. "*Christ*", I thought, "*I'm in a brothel manned by a child*". A door swung open, inside were five men sitting around playing a computer game. "Ah, not quite". I left back upstairs into the open daylight. Two conservatively dressed girls and a man smoking a cigarette leaned on a fence and stared at me in silence. I looked around and found the gym via a small entrance.

I had envisaged a dark room with rusty equipment manned by dodgy-looking blokes on steroids. But for the fact that I had to remove my shoes which I thought was a little unusual, not to mention dangerous, it was though refreshingly normal. I paid the entrance fee which I calculated to be USD$5 and which I thought was great value. Even more so when I worked out that I'd calculated it wrong, and it turned out to actually be USD$0.50. I bought a bottle of warm water stored in an unplugged fridge. It was peculiar to Uzbekistan, a largely desert country, that almost every fridge you come across is unplugged, presumably to save on power but which made it more of an expensive shelf rather than a fridge. I was the object of curiosity, as not only was I one of the few tourists in the city, almost certainly I had to have been one of the only non-Uzbeks to have ever visited this gym.

I rode back along the dusty road, stopping at a red light. Two louts not much older than myself pulled up next to me in a busted-up car, their arms hanging out the windows holding cigarettes. They looked both ways and with a screech of the tires, ripped across the major intersection ignoring the red light. "These bloody Uzbeks", I repeated to myself. Fifteen minutes later I arrived back at my hotel, handing the rusted broken bike to the lady I'd rented it from. She charged me 20,000 Uzbek Som for the hour and a bit I'd been gone, about as much as a public bike in the city of London.

*   *   *   *

I'd bought two carpets for two friends the day earlier and not wanting to lug rolled up carpets with my inconveniently full duffle bag, determined that I'd post them. My hotel manager explained that to avoid any issues with customs, I'd have to have them certified that they weren't antiquities, which meant taking them to a local city official. He kindly accompanied me to the building where this official in his large office, with his secretary at one end, were sitting. "Ah, welcome, welcome", this man said to me as he slapped me on the back. The friendliness seemed superficial. I unfurled the two carpets. "How much did you pay for them?" the official asked. I told him. "Great value, great value". My hotel manager appeared less sure. We filled out numerous forms for each one, all of which were stamped and signed by the official. Portraits of the current and past president looked down at me from the wall. And then an hour later, with the carpets now wrapped up tightly, and me slightly poorer, we left. My hotel manager pointed on a map where the post office was, which turned out to be at the end of a broken mud alleyway. Two big ladies with rows of gold teeth, dressed head to toe in 18th-century dress sat behind the counter, the only light coming from the grubby window and a single uncovered bulb. They were perfectly friendly, though neither spoke a lick of English. I filled out the forms, detailing the recipient and the sender using English characters despite the country using Cyrillic. After a significant amount of gesticulation, I handed the forms to the two ladies. Notwithstanding the tracking numbers they handed back to me, I was not feeling mightily confident as I left. I religiously checked those tracking numbers online over the following few weeks, but after a month of no updates, I sadly lost all hope. Until almost two months later when I received a picture message with a beaming friend holding up her carpet.

\*   \*   \*   \*

It was my final night in Bukhara, the food poisoning was subsiding, and I was feeling a little more refreshed. I wandered across to the Lyab-I Hauz*, a large rectangular pond in the centre of Bukhara surrounded by stone-built banks. The beautifully ornate 17th century Nadir Madrasah with its bright azure tiles depicting two phoenixes in flight peaked through the mulberry trees that had been growing for 500 years and were now draping into the water. Up until the 20th century, there were numerous hauzes such as this one through the city, all connected by small channels, and all fed from one much larger channel that led to the Zeravshan River. This river originated 600 km to the East, high up in the Pamir Mountains of Tajikistan, and after first passing through Samarkand, by the time it had reached Bukhara, it was nearing its end, petering out into this city and the desert beyond. Being at the 'end of the line' meant that once it reached Bukhara it would often run low with the ponds only being refreshed once a week, sometimes only a fortnight, at which point dirty citizens would make their way to the muddy banks and wash themselves. This became a breeding ground for diseases and the city became synonymous with the Sartian Sickness, the Bukhara Boil and perhaps most disgusting of all, the rishte worm. Armin Varbery, a Hungarian who in the mid-19th century passed through Bukhara in search of the origins of the Hungarian language, wrote in his 1864 book *Travels in Central Asia,* this of the worm:

---

*   Hauz meaning pond.

*One feels at first on the foot or on some other part of the body a tickling sensation, then a spot becomes visible whence issues a worm like a thread. This is often an ell long (roughly 80 cm), and it out some days after to be carefully would off on a reel. If the worm is broken off, an inflammation ensues, and instead of one, from six to ten make their appearance, which forces the patient to keep his bed for a week, subjecting him to intense suffering. The more courageous have the rishte cut out at the very beginning.*

As part of their drive to modernise and improve the living standards of the region, the Bolsheviks after arriving in the 1920s set about filling the hauzes in. All except this one.

I chose a restaurant at its edge and sat amongst the few tourists that were in the city sitting in couples with a hookah by their side, quietly talking amongst themselves as the sounds of an Uzbek busker filled the air. I had my book with me, *The Railway* by one of the few famous contemporary Uzbek writers—Hamid Ismailov. *"A wonderfully engaging novel"*, wrote the Financial Times, *"…an utterly readable, compelling book"*, the New Statesman, *"200 pages too long"*, me. With my train leaving at 3:15 am, and the train station at least half an hour away from where I was staying, I left early to pack my bags and grab a few hours' sleep.

My alarm went off at 2 am. I jumped into the clothes I'd laid out only a few hours earlier, grabbed my pre-packed bag and the envelope containing 160,000 Uzbeki Som (roughly USD$20) which I was going to give to Aziz, the hotel manager. I rushed downstairs, but instead of Aziz, it was his worker who I'd seen occasionally milling about the previous days. I gave him the envelope, told him to give it to Aziz, and then jumped into the pre-arranged taxi that was thankfully waiting for me nearby. We drove out of the city, past the now quiet domed bazaar, past the elegantly lit up madrassahs and out onto the long stretch of road to the train station.

I arrived at the train station and worked my way through the security, with the guards looking as sleepy as me. Inside the station were Uzbeks of various ages, some asleep, some quietly staring at me, and in the corner an older well-dressed American couple. I sat down and fired a message off to the hotel manager thanking him for his hospitality and making sure he knew about his tip. And then sat and waited for my extremely inconveniently timed train.

# KHIVA

The train from Bukhara to Khiva was to take seven hours and left Bukhara at 3:15 am. I had booked a sleeper room with two beds, for the grand total of USD$50 which, after walking the aisles of the train and passing families of Uzbeks crammed with crying children, I came to view as a screaming bargain. The station was relatively empty at that time of the morning with a few tired Uzbeks and a single old American couple. The train arrived punctually and we all walked back into the cold night and onto the train. Looking down at my ticket, written in Cyrillic, I couldn't for the life of me figure out which was my cabin and approached the conductor. He looked at it, nodded and pointed at one of the carriages. I boarded and paced the carriage looking for my room which didn't seem to exist. I approached another bloke who through gestures pointed out it was a different carriage which I swiftly bordered and again came unstuck. What the hell is going on I thought. On my third attempt with a different train staff, he led me to the front carriage and directed me into my room. Why had I been sent to the wrong carriage twice? "These bloody Uzbeks" I thought to myself. I found my room, and with the pitch black of night outside the train, lay down on my bed and rocked to sleep.

Waking early, three or so hours later, I pulled back the curtains to reveal a desert stretching into the horizon catching a glimpse of the morning sun. Needing to go to the bathroom—to urinate thank god—I rose and walked the length of the train. "Good morning", I said with a beaming smile to a large Uzbek babushka who stared directly back at me and grimaced. "How many god damn man bun wearing Australians have you seen on a train from Bukhara to Khiva at 6 am you ...", I happily thought to myself as I pushed past her and into the bathroom.

The sun was now fully up, illuminating a landscape marked with the occasional adobe building and roaming camel in the distance. I walked down to the dining car to have breakfast, clearly interrupting a couple of louts, who until I walked in, were laughing and smoking but now decided to stop and stare. Giving the old man acting as waiter a single USD$1, I ate my food and looked out at the unchanging landscape while the two louts continued to stare, one of them saying something in my direction, causing them both to burst into loud laughter. Feeling decidedly uncomfortable, I made my way back through the carriages, past Uzbeks staring out at me from their rooms, and back to my room where I closed the door and read, waiting for the stop in Khiva.

\*　　\*　　\*　　\*

It was late morning by the time I arrived into Khiva, and grabbing my bags, I jumped off the train and into the bustling crowd of people all vying for my fare. I nodded towards an old bloke grinning with a mouth full of gold, told him my address and agreed to his figure. That it was almost certainly double what I should've paid did not annoy me, it could've been triple and would still have been dirt cheap. What did annoy me was that his taxi service quickly became a bus service as the trip to my hotel turned into a trip around town with a few extra passengers.

I settled back into the seat of the car and accepted my fate at inadvertently becoming a part of Khiva's public transport and watched as one by one travellers were picked up and dropped off, all of whom expressed amused shock as they found me in the car. We finally dropped the last passenger to his home, a small poorly constructed one storey house sitting in the surrounding countryside. The roads out here had the surface evenness of a dry riverbed, testing the suspension of the car and the patience of its occupants. The countryside though came somewhat as a surprise. For the past seven hours, I had been chugging my way through a desert, with little in the way of vegetation and the only variation being the height of the sand dunes. Out here, however, the land was green and fertile as far as the eye could see, like a very large oasis. All a consequence of the Amu Darya river that cut north of Khiva, originating from a lake once named after Queen Victoria amongst the mountain ranges of Tajikistan, a thousand kilometres to the east. And a river that in Ancient Greece had been known as the River Oxus, that famous river which Alexander the Great had crossed as his decisive step into Central Asia. Once it had continued west and north, eventually emptying into and replenishing the Aral Sea. Now instead, it simply peters out and dribbles across the land, feeding huge cotton plantations built by the Soviets, a crop not known for its lack of thirst.

We didn't stick around here for long though—our driver had passengers to drop off (namely me)—and turned back towards Khiva proper. As the countryside disappeared once again into the squat poorly built buildings that made up Khiva's suburbs, we were made to stop briefly as an Uzbeki woman hurriedly loaded her shopping into the boot of a parked taxi. For my driver, this was an outrage, and he decided to make it known by slamming his hand on the horn from the moment we arrived, to which she responded by shooting *me* a sharp look. A full thirty seconds of horn later, we were moving again. Getting lost in what seemed to me a straightforward route, my driver stopped at a hotel outside the old city of Khiva to ask for directions. Pointing out that he had gone the wrong way, the driver began insisting I walk the remainder which I ignored and jumped back into the car. I could feel the tension from the driver, as we weaved through streets and back onto the direction of my hotel, obviously irritated that he had to do his job. I stared out of the window. We were driving around the perimeter of the old city, marked by well-preserved city walls with crenelated tops and steep banks, which made for an awesome and formidable sight. There were four entry gates, each flanked by large guard towers. Our entrance was the Southern gate through whose narrow entrance we gingerly directed our car, as the guard towers and arch loomed large above us. Tarmac turned to a hardened earth, and the relative openness of the town outside of the gates changed to tightly packed sand-coloured buildings, with minarets offering splashes of colour in the sky. Finally, 12 hours after leaving Bukhara, I had stepped into the ancient city of Khiva.

\* \* \* \*

The story of this city was a familiar one, like those of the other cities in the region. Established roughly 2.5 millennium ago, conquered by Alexander the Great, followed by the Arab armies, conquered by Genghis Khan, and later destroyed and pillaged by the Uzbek's National Hero, Tamerlane. The city's true historic significance came after all of this, however, when the Uzbeks spread down from the north, filling the power vacuum left by Tamerlane's demise. For once the Uzbeks had established themselves across modern Uzbekistan and Tajikistan, the region split into four different controlling entities, with one taking Khiva as its capital and adopting its name to become the Khanate of Khiva. This Khanate controlled what would now be southern Kazakhstan, western

Uzbekistan and much of Turkmenistan, along with almost the entire east coast of the Caspian Sea and much of the Aral Sea. It was under this new era starting in the 16th century, that the city began to flourish, becoming a staging post for Central Asia trade and a recipient of taxes from across huge tracts of land. But where it really made its mark was in establishing itself as the epicentre of the human slave trade.

\*     \*     \*     \*

The city lies on the edge of the Karakum desert, a 350,000 square kilometre desert that spreads south across Turkmenistan until it reaches the mountains that today separate Turkmenistan from Iran. During this 'golden age' of Khiva, it was roamed by Turkmen nomads whose principle source of wealth came from capturing and selling people. Often, those captured would be Persians which the Turkmens would link up in chain gangs and then march hundreds of kilometres across desert to Khiva, suffering an awful attrition rate. Once in Khiva, those that had survived would be led to the Khivan slave market, the largest in Central Asia, where they would be auctioned off. Arriving in 1863 and disguised as a whirling dervish (a Sufi), Armin Vambery recorded the prices paid for slaves to be around £21-£36 (in 1863 money), though this would drop to less than a tenth if there was a particularly large bounty of slaves.

This slave trade was overseen and approved by the ruling Khan himself, who took the title of Kharzem which meant 'Rejoicing in War'. And seeing himself as the great protector and enforcer of the faith, he believed that it was his duty to punish with the greatest severity any offense against it. While in Khiva, Vambery was invited to his court and was made to witness the punishment served upon some Turkomen raiders who a week earlier had murdered a Khivan caravan. Quoting directly from his account:

> *"Whilst several were led to the gallows or the block, I saw how, at a sign from the executioner, eight aged men placed themselves down on their back upon the earth. They were then bound hand and foot, and the executioner gouged out their eyes in turn, kneeling to do so on the breast of each poor wretch; and after every operation he wiped his knife, dripping with blood, upon the white beard of the hoary unfortunate".*

But it was this trade in slaves, and more particularly the trade in Russian slaves, that expedited the fall of the Khivan Khanate. For the huge number of Russian slaves that had accumulated and been traded within the walls of Khiva made a compelling reason for the Russian Empire to enter the fray. That it suited their geopolitical machinations at the time was somewhat convenient.

And so only ten years after Vambery had snuck into the city in disguise at preposterous risk to his life, Khiva fell to the Russian forces which changed Khivan life, almost at once, rather dramatically. All diplomatic and military control was seceded to the Russian Empire, the Khanate was opened to Russian merchants and slavery was once and for all abolished. A change that was illustrated nicely by the British colonel Frederick Burnarby's entrance into the city in 1876, a mere 13 years after Vamerby's. Where he was warmly welcomed by the now subdued Khan and invited to share in glasses of champagne, the Khan pointing out that champagne hadn't been known to the prophet and he, therefore, would not have laid down any laws prohibiting its use.

Sadly 142 years later there were no longer any Khans to share a champagne with, but his ark was still there, so having checked into my hotel, I set out in search of it.

*   *   *   *

I set my sights on a brightly coloured minaret in the distance and set off in its general direction. The streets were of hardened earth that separated ancient-looking rudimentary houses seemingly made of adobe and wood. But for the occasional tourist, the streets were largely empty, for unlike Bukhara which functioned as a city, Khiva was more of an open-air museum, though one which saw few visitors. The minaret loomed larger as I reached the main street, with merchants now lining either side, selling their trinkets to the few tourists meandering about. A camel sat in the shade of a tree, chewing its cud, indifferent to the passing traffic.

At the end of this street stood the foundations of what was intended to have been the tallest minaret in the world. Construction had begun in the 19th century when the Khan, in a fit of penis insecurity, decided that he wanted the tallest minaret in the world, so tall that he would be able to see Bukhara from it's top. It was never completed because—so the rumour goes—the Khan ordered the architect thrown from its top after discovering he had intended to build an even bigger one in Bukhara. More likely, it came to an end when the Khan died thereby ending his expensive glory project. Still, at 15 m wide and 29 m tall, and covered in vivid turquoise and majolica tiles*, the Kalta Minor Minaret is impressive and is arguably *the* symbol of Khiva.

It was difficult to fully comprehend Khiva amongst these tightly packed streets, so I wandered across to a rather plain looking minaret to see whether I could climb it. And it turned out I could! Though to get to the top, I needed to first enter the Djuma Mosque, a three-century-old single-story mosque, supported by 212 intricately carved ancient wooden columns. The mosque was dimly lit but for light pouring through an opening in the ceiling, creating a glorious effect as the shadows of each column stretched across the mosque's earthen floor. A small door in the mosque's side marked the entrance to the minaret and paying a small fee, I crouched through and began climbing.

The tight spiralling staircase, with uneven stairs and ceiling, made me duck and twist as I rose steadily through its column. Small horizontal slits allowed for just enough light to prevent me from tripping but did nothing to alleviate the feeling of claustrophobia. But having climbed the 57 m,

---

* An Italian style of ceramic that creates brilliant translucent colours.

sometimes on hands and knees, I reached its open-air domed top. With a light wind coming through the gaps, I sat down next to two pigeons who were eyeing me suspiciously and looked out across Khiva. The city was stuck too far in the past for the silence to be interrupted by an engine, and the minaret too high to capture the voices of the people below.

Below me sat the Matpana Baya Madrassah, which had operated as an Islamic school before the Bolsheviks arrived and converted it into a Museum of Atheism. Hundreds of these atheism museums had been set up across the Soviet Union, spearheaded by a Communist group named the *League of Militant Atheists* under the motto "The Storming of Heaven"! After the Soviet Union collapsed, the museum lost its 'Atheism' theme though it was confusingly hard to tell what theme replaced it. When I visited the following day, I saw one display showing a two bodied, one headed sheep with a plaque underneath simply stating 'Ugly Sheep'.

Behind the Madrassah though, and buttressed against the city walls, sat the city's Ark where 155 years earlier, Humbery had watched an eye-gouging, and 13 years later, where Burnaby had sat and shared a glass of champagne. And so, gingerly climbing back down the minaret, I set off in its direction.

*     *     *     *

A crenelated wall fortified the ark, with a large gate flanked by two guard towers acting as the entrance. Inside, the complex was divided into different sections, the first upon entry being where the city's troops had once trained and paraded. It was here too where executions took place, presumably making it the spot Humbery had sat all those years earlier. Different areas within the Ark joined here and led to the Ark's prison, the stables and the armoury. I carried on through one of the openings and into the reception area that had once welcomed delegates visiting the Khan. At its centre stood a large circular stone where the Khan would set up yurts in honour of visiting nomadic dignitaries. And to its side stood a large hall open at one side and held up by two tall wooden pillars, each carved in patterns and poems. The inside of the hall was beautifully decorated with complicated Islamic patterns, all in various shades of blue glinting in the light, giving the feeling of standing in a jewellery box. It was here where the Khan would sit on his throne and be addressed by those visitors, possibly too where he sat and had a champagne with Barnaby. That silver-plated throne was no longer here, long ago taken to the Kremlin's Armory in Moscow where it sits today.

I had read of a spot in Khiva that was perfect to watch the sun set over this ancient city, and as the sky was beginning to turn an ochre red, I set out in search of it. I didn't have to walk far though, as that spot was on top of the ark, where its fortified walls joined into the walls surrounding the city. I climbed to the top of the wall and looked across the city. The minarets and madrassahs were sending long shadows across the sand-coloured buildings, and in the distance, I could see smoke drifting lazily from the chimneys of houses sitting amongst the surrounding fertile fields. Though beyond that I could just make out the sand dunes that marked the beginning of the Karakum Desert, where once caravans of slaves would emerge from to be sold amongst the buildings below me.

*     *     *     *

A few days later I woke for an early breakfast and waited for the patriarch of the hotel to take me to the border with Turkmenistan, a trip that I felt a little trepidatious about. I became more trepidatious when the time my man was to pick me up came and went. I started speaking with the girl behind the front desk, initially asking where the hell her father was. She was 18, she had just finished school and had applied to Urgench University, just outside of Khiva. "That's great, and what about travel, are you intending to travel outside of Uzbekistan", "No", came the quick reply. What type of culture breeds smart multi-lingual kids who have no curiosity about the outside world I wondered? The father arrived, 45 minutes late without explanation, simply grinning his gold teeth filled mouth and off we went, along a bumpy highway to the border.

I watched out the window as we cut through vast fields of cotton, passing numerous large trucks and machinery all bearing Chinese writing, and eventually arrived at the border. I thanked my driver and hopped out of the car as he and his car sped off back down the road kicking up dust in his wake. I looked at my phone to see an email from the hotel in Bukhara where I'd been days earlier. The manager had sent me a message. [sic] *"Good day dear Christopher !! i hope you could get your night time train on time . i will be glad to see you next time in Bukhara/About tip for me---i was surprised when you said you left it with my colleague... because he didn't give me anything . i asked him about your tip he said you gave it to him and it belongs to him . i didn't try to persuade him to share with me just told him to keep it. may be next time when you will be in bukhara you leave tip with me directly".* [sic]

"These bloody Uzbeks", I thought to myself one last time.

# TURKMENISTAN

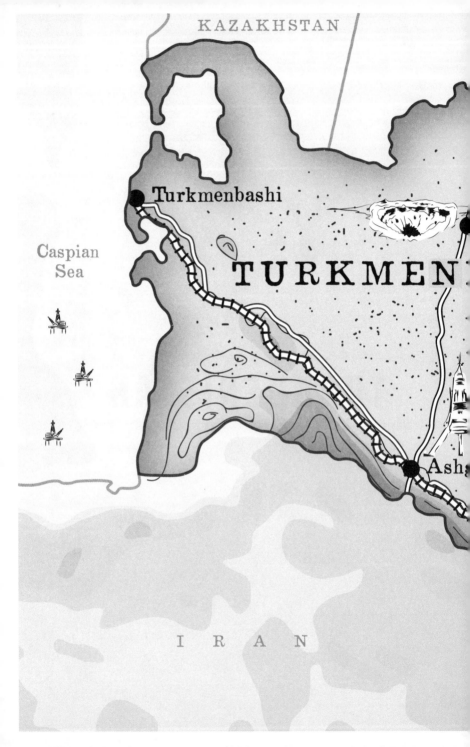

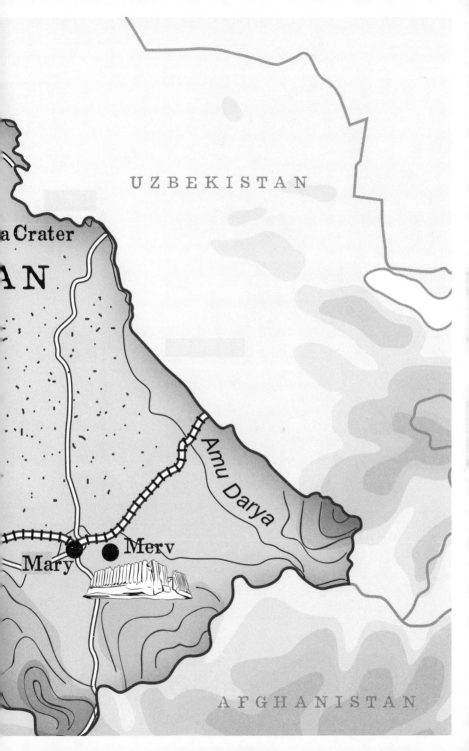

'North Korea—but with money'—should be *the* tourist slogan for Turkmenistan, and could go towards capturing some of the 6,000 tourists that visit that lovely country each year, thereby doubling its own. My plan to make a dent in the tourism industry was to enter the country via the north, passing through one of the three land crossings that Turkmenistan and Uzbekistan share along their 1,800 km stretch of border. I had read that this crossing was 'intimidating for those who are not used to these kinds of crossings', which along with accounts of arbitrary bag searches, misclassifying of flu tablets as hard drugs and all-around general unpleasantness, meant I had hopped out of bed that day with a high degree of apprehension. The day I arrived however it was empty, and on either side, it was rather routine. The only thing that really marked this as slightly different than your average crossing was the 1.5 km barbed wire no man's land that I crossed alone but for one old bloke coming the other direction. I gave him a friendly "Hi mate", to which he gave a silent nod back. It felt like I was in some sort of spy thriller whereby I was being swapped for another spy, though it was rather hard to picture the geopolitical situation resulting in the swap of a 33-year-old New Zealander with that of a 75+-year-old Turkmen. I carried on along this tract of no man's land, crossing from one ostensibly democratic country into another, where the President of Turkmenistan had somewhat recently won the election with a landslide 97.69% of the vote. Which makes you wonder who those 2.31% were and reminds you of the Azerbaijani elections in 2013 where it was announced that the incumbent president had won 73% of the vote... the day before the election.

\*　　\*　　\*　　\*

Turkmenistan, the second most isolated country in the world after North Korea, run by the second of two megalomaniac dictators to grace this country, the first pushing past Kim Jong Un—who, let me remind you, scored 17 of 18 holes in one the first time he played golf—in the league of absurdity. Having been appointed Soviet strong man of the country by Mikhail Gorbachev in 1985, by the time the USSR had collapsed in 1991, Saparmyrat Nyyazow had assumed control and went on to lead the country for what turned out to be a hilarious (from the outside) 15 years. Along with changing the word for 'bread' and the month of April to his mother's name, Mr. Nyyazow, President for Life and self-styled "Father of the People" went on to:

* Name a city, brand of vodka, a type of tea, two kinds of cologne and a meteorite after himself;

* Forbid makeup on Turkmen women after reportedly not being able to tell the difference between the sexes;

* Forbid the listening to car stereos by Turkmen men;

* Banned the ballet, opera and circus for being 'un-Turkmen';

* Outlawed long hair and beards;

* Decreed that childhood lasted until 13, adolescence until 25, youth until 37 and that old age didn't begin until 85.

* And... wrote the 'Ruhnama', a book he declared to be so good that he awarded himself the National Award for Excellence and insisted on it being placed in every school classroom, and alongside the Koran in every Mosque.

Unsurprisingly, a few imams saw this last move as giving the Ruhnama equal stature as that of the word of God and therefore rather blasphemous. However, since Mr. Nyyazow saw himself as a God, he understandably had those Imams Mosques blown up. Moreover, and due to the absolute divine nature of his word, he had a copy of it pushed from a Russian spacecraft's airlock so that it would sit orbiting the Earth for the next 150 years. Though it's hard to say whether this last point is stranger than the fact that he had statues of the Ruhnama placed around the capital, to mechanically open during certain times of the day to play recorded extracts through loudspeakers.

But I wasn't here to find the birthplace of the Ruhnama: The Book of Soul, that was strangely (according to Google) liked by 60% of Google Users. I was here to get to the ancient city of Merv, the *extremely* bizarre capital of Ashgabat but first to the Darvasa Crater.

# THE DARVASA CRATER

The Darvasa Crater is a football field-sized hole in the ground, surrounded by sand dunes, in the centre of Turkmenistan and is nicknamed 'The Gates to Hell'. To get here, I'd just spent five hours bouncing along a pot-holed highway, with shrubby dunes on either side preventing the view of even a horizon. Having spent a week in the Isle of Wight, I'd been to holes before, but this one was slightly and infamously different. It had accidentally formed when Soviet engineers looking for oil in the region had drilled into a cavity of natural gas, collapsing the ground beneath them and swallowing up their heavy machinery in the process. This collapse set off a small chain reaction, opening holes across the landscape, and more significantly creating vents for methane to escape into the atmosphere. Methane isn't poisonous—I would've been dead on arrival following my train ride into Khiva had it been—but it does replace the oxygen in the air and can, therefore, be lethal due to suffocation. Recognising this, the Soviet scientists thought that the best approach would be to burn off the escaping methane which they estimated would finish it off in a few weeks. That was in 1971, and the fire that they started almost fifty years ago has been burning ever since.

"What a waste, surely all that gas and heat could be used for something", which I thought was a perfectly reasonable suggestion but which my guide found offensive, perhaps because I was suggesting destroying one of the country's few tourist sites. My guide's name was Emil, and she had picked me up five hours earlier from the Uzbekistan Turkmenistan border and had initially toured me through the ancient city of Konye-Urgench. Like many cities in the region, it had felt the fury of Genghis Khan when he swept through in 1221 destroying the city and murdering its inhabitants. And after just over a century of pulling itself back together, it was dealt a second punch by Genghis's descendant Tamerlane, who massacred the city's population, destroyed its buildings and then tore down the dams that were irrigating the surrounding landscape, thereby flooding it and turning it into marshland. The city never recovered and, in its place, today stands a 60 m tall 900-year-old minaret and an equally ancient mausoleum, both impressive on scale and beauty but now simply lone monuments standing in a gravesite that was once a city. With that being all there really was however, we'd breezed through and then eventually arrived at the crater.

"Well, I think it's beautiful", Emil said in response. I agreed with her somewhat I suppose. We had been at the site for at least an hour and in that time the sun had started to dip allowing the colour of the flames to only grow brighter against the landscape. Every now and then a wind would sweep through and whip up the flames, causing a hot drought to swirl around you and capture you in its heat, giving a sense of raw power. Ultimately though it was a hole in the ground with flames coming out of it and I quickly shot down Emil's suggestion that we wait another couple of hours to allow the sun to drop below the horizon. Emil was disappointed, but the driver clearly wasn't, and so we jumped back in the car, made our way through the dunes and eventually onto the broken highway. This time we were heading to the capital of the country, and perhaps one of the most bizarre cities in the world, Ashgabat.

# ASHGABAT

We live in Paradise. A Turkmen saying says that when you die you go to heaven and end up in Ashgabat", explained Emil. To be fair, the capital—Ashgabat, is pristine and impressive. Though impressive in an absolute downright bloody mad weirdness. The entire city is made of white Italian marble, every car—by law—is white, there are more fountains than in Las Vegas, and at one end stands the enormous 'Arch of Neutrality' with a statue of the first president ('President for Life') made of pure gold standing atop with arms outstretched to the population, that used to slowly rotate throughout the day always facing the sun. At the other, a Monument to the Future with a large model of a Carbon atom surrounded by eight flying saucers/UFOs. The Ministry of Dentistry building is in the shape of a tooth, the Ministry of Oil and Gas, a cigarette lighter, the

Ministry of Foreign Affairs topped with an extremely gaudy version of the Earth. "Thank god we don't have a Ministry of Gynaecology" joked Emil. And like some Orwellian nightmare, sitting atop a hill overlooking the city is the Palace of Happiness where locals come to get married under the warm embrace of the government. Much like Astana to the north, this was a city that had been dreamt up by a dictator, suddenly shed of his Soviet overlords and flush with hydrocarbon dollars, willing to enact his singular vision of a Utopia.

*     *     *     *

Ashgabat had originally been founded by the Russians following their destruction of the nearby Turkmen fort of Geok-Tepe and the defeat of the Turkmen army. The Silk Road had run directly through the Turkmen lands and for years, the Turkmens had led raiding parties on those passing caravans and Russian outposts further to the north, forcing those they captured into slavery. Thousands of young Russian women became Turkmen brides in this way, and it was rumoured that the captured men would have iron rungs looped around their collar bone to stop them from escaping. Those that did attempt to escape but were caught would have their feet chopped off. This outrage along with growing anxiety about British influence to the south of modern-day Turkmenistan, pushed the Russians to decide it was now time to solve these two issues once and for all. And so, in 1879 General Lomakin marched 4,000 Russian troops from their base on the Caspian Sea to the Turkmen fortress of Geok-Tepe, with the purpose of destroying the fortress, freeing the Russian slaves and taking control of the region.

Coming on the back of military success against the Ottomans, and eager for a swift victory, Lomakin rushed his assault by halting his artillery barge too early and storming the fort too soon. The Turkmen, who though substantially unarmed, significantly outnumbered the Russians, and with their defences still intact, overwhelmed the attackers, killing close to a quarter of them and capturing many more. The surviving Russians fled back into the desert but were picked off in their retreat by the Turkmen now armed with the dead Russians guns. This failed assault was to be Russia's worst defeat in the region since their failed attempt at capturing Khiva in 1717, and came to be known throughout Europe as the 'Lomakin massacre'.

Eager for revenge, in 1881 the Russians made a second assault of Geok-Teppe. This time around, they arrived with a significantly larger army that included 20 times the artillery and almost twice the number of infantry and perhaps most importantly, included the leadership of a much more ruthless general. A distinguished General, Mikhail Skobelev had been killing Central Asians since he had been sent to Tashkent in 1868. Said to chase danger almost as eagerly as he chased women, he was described by one British Field Marshal as the world's "ablest single commander" and by a Russian contemporary as "the God of War personified". And so, on arriving to Geok-Tepe at the age of 37, he decided that instead of storming the fortress—a strategy that had failed during the first attempt—he would undertake a full-scale siege. For up to a month he besieged the city, before ingeniously having his Russian sappers' tunnel underneath the walls of the Geok-Tepe fortress, detonating a mine and ordering his infantry to swarm in through the newly formed hole. What followed was a full-scale slaughter of the Turcmen population, an orgy of rape, looting and violence that saw the killing of between 25,000 and 40,000 inhabitants. Citizens that had in the final moments decided to finally evacuate the city and flee into the desert were chased down and killed by the Russian cavalry. With such a distance between this battle and the chattering classes of Europe, this could easily have been presented as a swift success, and a rehabilitation of Russia's image in Europe, so sorely bruised by its defeat two years earlier. Unbeknownst to the Russians however, an Irish reporter for the London Daily News had been sitting 12 miles east on the top of a hill, watching the massacre unfold through the lens of his binoculars. "No one was spared, not even young children or the elderly. All were mercilessly cut down by Russian sabres", shouted the London Daily News, all too happy to cast the Russians in a negative light. A British Viceroy to India later described the fall of this city as "not a route, but a massacre; not a defeat but an extirpation". General Skobelev dug his heels in though; "I hold it as a principle that the duration of the peace is in direct proportion to the slaughter you inflict upon the enemy. The harder you hit them, the longer they remain quiet". While happy at the success of his assault, the Russians bowed to pressure and relieved General Skobelev of his post.

This incident became a national tragedy for the Turkmen who were defeated, massacred and lost control of their territory, and who since Independence from the Soviet Union in 1990 had held the day of the defeat—12 January—as a national day of memory. That was until recently when the President without explanation 'merged' this day with another public holiday, a move many regarded as a nod to the Kremlin whom they no longer wish to offend. Either way, what was a catastrophe for the Turkmen was a success for the Russians who had successfully conquered what is now modern-day Turkmenistan and established a buffer against the British to their south. Though with British-influenced Persia some 50 km to the south of Geok-Teppe, the Russians determined that a new fort would be needed and so in 1881 established Ashgabat.

\*    \*    \*    \*

For my first morning in Ashgabat Emil took me to the Turkmenbashi Ruhy Mosque. The largest mosque in Central Asia, built to the cost of $100 million, located at the site of where the First President was born, and given a name translating to "The Mosque of Turkmenbashi Spirituality", a mosque almost certainly not in dedication to Allah. The structure itself—all in white marble of course—was spread across 18 million square metres and surrounded by waterways and fountains designed to reflect the sky and give the impression the mosque was floating. Underneath the mosque sat an underground car park, making it easy to visit for the 10,000 worshippers that the place could hold. It was a slow day the day we arrived however, as the only other person across this sprawling 18 million square metre landscape was a single lone guard. "Where is everyone, why isn't anyone here?" "Because it's a busy workday", came the unconvincing answer. We passed by the guard and into the entrance of the grounds which happened to be the Turkmenbashi Mausoleum containing the First President himself lying in a sarcophagus alongside his mother and two brothers. Black granite slabs served as the coffins and a white marble statue of an angel holding Turkmenbashi (presumably delivering him to heaven) stood to one side. The book of Ruhmani sat at the centre, really driving home the point that he had considered this more divine than the Quran, equally illustrating the point at how mad he was. We stepped back out into the sun and walked our way up the Italian marble steps to the mosque, passing synchronised fountains at either side spraying precious water into the desert air.

"Ah damn, it's closed", I exclaimed to Emil as we approached the two-story-high large wooden doors, which looked to be locked. She ignored me and leaning against one of the doors pushed it slowly open with a creak that echoed through the empty cavernous structure.

Taking our shoes off and placing them by the door, we made our way to the centre of the building walking across what felt like a cloud and happened to be one of the largest handmade rugs in the world. I followed Emil in step as she reached the centre of the room, lay down on her back and looked up at the centre of the dome. Surrounding the inside of the dome were the words of the Ruhmani. "Have you read it?" I asked. "Oh yeah, it's very good. It's helped me through tough times", Emil responded never taking her eyes off the text. While the book was recently brushed aside from national prominence as an embarrassing quirk of the First President's leadership, up until 2013 it had been required reading for the average Turkmen. Public servants would periodically be tested on their knowledge of it, and for any hope of advancing through the ranks, a thorough understanding of it was essential. And as for the country's students, the first 15 minutes of every subject taught started with reading from its passages. For Emil, who at 28 would've finished school in 2008, this meant that like her peers she had been brought up with the Ruhmani for a good part of her formative years. Which explained her defensive adulation for it, though like with much of the things she told me that were plainly absurd, there was a hesitation, something that suggested she wasn't entirely convinced by her indoctrination.

We rose from the carpet and made our way back out with Emil gingerly closing the large wooden door behind us. But for the quiet splashing of the water from the fountains, the grounds remained still and silent. We exited back through the Mausoleum, walking again past the bodies of the First President and his family. In the hour we had been gone, our driver had fallen asleep presumably unable to distract himself with books (partly banned), cigarettes (effectively banned) or social media (completely banned). The guard who had welcomed us had since disappeared, so as I gazed back across the vast complex, with the largest Central Asian mosque glistening in the sun, surrounded by fountains spraying synchronised jets of clean water into the dry air, I could see no one. One massive mausoleum built by the man who it was dedicated to sitting alone in the desert, being visited by the ever-occasional New Zealander. "Look on my works ye mighty…" it seemed to say.

*   *   *   *

All of which was starting to become a little disconcerting. It was late morning by now and I had interacted in some way with a grand total of four people, and that included an unspeaking waitress at breakfast. Thankfully, the next destination included "People's Memorial" in its name, which gave me some hope that I would at least see people wandering around. For like other public grounds around the world, this was presumably built after much due diligence, cost-benefit analysis and public consultation, to ensure that if money was to be spent from the public purse, it would at least be spent on the owners of that purse. And I was right…

…For when I arrived, I instantly saw two people. It didn't matter that they were guards, and rather than wandering around were standing in glass boxes out in the midday sun, for there was no doubt that there were multiple other guards spying me from a distance.

I was standing at the top of the Halk Hakydasy "People's Memorial", a memorial that had recently been built in memory of the three major events to shape modern Turkmenistan: The Geok-Tepe defeat that had delivered the country from the Turkmen to the Russians, the 1948 earthquake that had levelled the Russian built Ashgabat and the 'Great Patriotic War' (World War 2) that the Turkmen had been pulled into on behalf of the Russians. The complex was made up of a large park that cascaded down the slope of a hill towards Ashgabat sitting in the distance. Well-watered and symmetrically placed trees lined a long perfectly clean concrete staircase that ran down its centre, leading from a highway at the staircase's bottom up to the centrepiece of the memorial complex at its top. The memorial complex was made up of a large eight-pointed star platform, with three considerable sculptures at opposing points. The central display were five 27-metre-high steles surrounding an eternal flame, in memory of the Turkmen soldiers of World War 2. To its right, a large masonry arch with three bronze figures, a woman at the centre and two soldiers at either side of her with their heads bowed, in memory of the Turkmen defeat by the Russians at Goek-Tepe. And opposite this, atop a large granite block stood a giant bronze bull, its horns holding a symbolically shattered Earth. And from the Earth, a woman, captured in a moment of falling while throwing her arms up in a desperate attempt to save the boy held in her hands.

The 1948 Earthquake memorialised by this statue, known in Turkmenistan as 'The Catastrophe' was so devastating that it levelled 98% of Ashgabat and killed two thirds of its population. The survivors were forced to sign non-disclosure agreements preventing them from discussing the event, part of the USSR's paranoid veil of secrecy, which meant that the world didn't find out about this tragedy until the days of Perestroika. Thankfully from all of this though emerged the country's saviour—the First President himself. For while his family died in the Earthquake, notably his mother and brothers whom I'd passed by in the Mausoleum moments earlier—he survived and went on to create the great nation of Turkmenistan, and of course the Ruhmani. Which explained why the boy in the woman's arms above me was made of solid gold. This was no longer the official explanation of the statue, however, and the boy now represented all Turkmen as they emerged from the Earthquake stronger than before, but Emil made sure I knew who the boy really characterized. That the official line had since changed was one more example of the ongoing expunging of the previous President's embarrassing past. And while the current President was having some success, no doubt to the relief of many Turkmen, some things were harder to erase from the city than others, especially when they were 95 metres tall and shaped like a three-legged rocket.

\*   \*   \*   \*

That three-legged gold and white 1970s retro-future styled building was the 'Arch of Neutrality', built by the First President in celebration of the country's policy of 'permanent neutrality'. A vague and poorly articulated policy designed by the First President, that essentially meant Turkmenistan wouldn't join a side in anyone else's conflict, nor join any alliances. It is a policy that the Turkmenistan government happily promotes to the Turkmen people as an example of their pioneering leadership on the world stage. From the perspective of the international community however, it is a policy that has allowed Turkmenistan to sit on the sidelines of world affairs, shielding it from outside pressure to liberalise. Either way, the First President was rather proud of it, and as a testament to it, built the Arch of Neutrality. That he also placed a 12-metre-tall gold-plated statue of himself on top of it that rotated throughout the day so that it always faced the sun, suggested that he was rather proud of himself too. Sadly, the new President put a stop to this, and in fact disassembled the structure, before rebuilding it on the outskirts of the city. The statue still exists, but it now has the dishonour of sometimes not facing the sun.

We parked in one of the empty car parks at the base of the Arch, which sat a short drive along empty highways from the "People's Memorial". The huge monument stood overhead, its long shadow protecting us from the sun as Emil and I approached one of the three legs which contained the elevators to take us to the top. A man was waiting in the elevator, surprisingly unsurprised to see us, and with the three of us on board, quietly pressed the button to take us up. The elevator slid on an angle up the leg and opened into the complex inside the arch, a man jumping up from his seat to greet us.

Emil indicated for me to follow her through the complex, stopping in front of various golden trophies covered in shiny gems, each encased in glass boxes. These trophies were gifts to the First President Emil explained, all implying the high-status people felt for him. That the trophies had been given and presented to him by the various government departments that he controlled didn't seem to weigh on Emil's mind. Another man appeared as if from nowhere but didn't say anything, other than to indicate we couldn't take photos. We continued around the circular structure until we reached the open-air viewing platform that allowed us to look down and across the city. Below us were the empty car parks amongst the vast pristine grounds, all filled with luscious grass and trees, with clean walkways amongst them forming geometric shapes. Two cafes sat opposite one another, both with chairs and tables confidently laid out. There was no one sitting at these chairs though, in fact, the only indication of anyone around were the two cars in the car park, one of which was ours. And spread out in the distance was the city of Ashgabat, a vast array of white marble buildings, all glittering in the sun. Separating them were long empty motorways, occupied by the occasional car. And not unlike Dubai, in the empty gaps sat a desert landscape. Not entirely desert though, for amongst the sand there stood literally thousands of adolescent trees, all in perfect rows like out of the game Sim City. This was a result of the current President's ambition to plants millions of trees thereby engineering the desert landscape and in turn its climate to be more hospitable, something that I find rather bold and admirable. That it involved 281,000 'volunteers' including thousands of school children whose school days were cut short, less so.

*    *    *    *

It was early afternoon by now which called for lunch. For the past few weeks, I had almost solely eaten heavy soups and meaty dishes, only few vegetables and not a single serving of fish. The drastic change in my diet was taking its toll on my bowels, where I was having to juggle between drugs that insured things would remain appropriately inside, with others to set off a quick evacuation. So, when Emil asked what I wanted for lunch, in a Hail Mary move I suggested sushi. That the nearest ocean was literally thousands of kilometres away didn't bother me, for this was Turkmenistan which on a GDP per capita basis was ostensibly richer than Brazil, China and South Africa. Surely, they were flying fresh fish in by the planeload to feed their rich countrymen. And clearly, my reasoning was correct, as Emil—albeit after some hesitation—agreed. And to my pleasure explained that it was located inside a shopping mall which presumably meant I was *finally* about to see people.

We parked our car in an empty car park and entered the shopping mall to a crowd of almost no one. Most of the shops were closed and of those that were open, none were playing music which combined with the broken escalators meant the place was eerily silent. Large pictures of the smiling President hung from the ceiling, doing no favours to the atmosphere.

We trudged our way up the broken escalators to the top floor where our sushi restaurant was sitting in a food court. The two people behind the counter were shocked to see me, though I wondered whether they were simply shocked to see anyone. I let Emil know what I wanted who then translated this to the staff. "Nope, no fish... they have miso though". Damnit. I ordered what I could and sat down to deep-fried chicken, bowls of rice with soy sauce and miso soup. A picture of the First President, beaming a happy smile, hung close by staring down at us. I asked Emil about the state of politics in her country, sensitive to the fact that this was somewhat of a police state and that any unwanted questioning could lead to trouble for me, or more likely Emil. I began gently.

"Was Gurbanguly (The First President) a good guy?"

"Oh yeah, he was amazing for Turkmenistan..." Emily responded before going on to list the various building projects built on his watch. "And as you saw with his policy of neutrality, he brought us international respect".

"A few of the things I've read about him seemed somewhat excessive", I offered.

"That was because he received bad advice. A lot of the people around him were very corrupt" came the response, which was the exact same response I'd heard from someone once defending Mao.

We had finished lunch and wandered back down the broken escalators and out into the car. Without the Big Brother-like picture of the First President staring down at me, I felt a little more comfortable pressing more firmly on Emil.

"With all the restrictions that your Presidents have created, it sort of seems like they're, well… dictators".

"The President is limited to 7-year terms", Emil curtly shot back, "and besides what difference does it make? In the West all the politicians are corrupt anyway, it's just the same".

For the first time, I could sense tension forming between us so decided against pressing further.

We were nearing my hotel, where I had decided to have dinner that night. The strain on my bowels was wearing me down, and I felt like an early dinner and simply reading all evening, not to mention exploring the cavernous but empty hotel. In any normal circumstance, I probably would've gone for an evening stroll but that was impossible in Ashgabat which required that I be confined to my hotel without a government chaperone.

Before dropping me off, Emil asked whether, along with the various national monuments we'd be visiting the following day, all of which sounded riveting, was there anything else I wanted to visit. "Yes actually, a café…. A busy one please", I asked. Emil thought for a moment, nodded and said farewell.

\*   \*   \*   \*

Prior to entering the country, I'd read that hotel rooms were monitored, something I'd experienced years ago in Pyongyang when my hotel room had a security camera inconspicuously aimed at my bed. In this hotel room, but for the décor there was nothing openly untoward but I couldn't help wondering whether someone was monitoring me as I sat there straining on the toilet seat. I made myself a coffee and opened the curtains to the view of the city at morning. The streets were entirely empty and the only movement came from the large billboards which showed the President wearing national garb holding a white puppy, with a digital Turkmen flag flapping in the background.

*    *    *    *

I met with Emil in the lobby and wandered outside. It was only early morning but the temperature was already nearing 30 degrees. We headed off to the café, driving through pristine streets, past shining white marble gold-trimmed buildings and fountains putting on shows to no one. That there were no pedestrians could be put down to the heat, that there were almost no cars either was put down to everyone being at work, according to Emil. She pointed out a stadium with an enormous horse head sitting at its top—said to be the biggest horse head in the world. It had been built along with the surrounding grounds at a massive cost to the country that couldn't afford it, for the 10-day 2017 Asian Indoor and Martial Arts. State workers made 'voluntary' contributions to the cost, which were automatically deducted from their pay checks, and the subsidised cost of water, gas and electricity all came to an end following the complex's construction. Some of that money went to a sophisticated and modern monorail sitting above the grounds but which, as we glided past in our car, sat motionless.

Our driver dropped us off at the base of what looked to be a low-slung office building and which Emil insisted contained a café. In the distance, I noticed a couple strolling along a street, the woman dressed in a beautiful green traditional dress, but as soon as I saw them, they were gone again. It was back to simply Emil and I. We wandered up the steps of the building onto its unshaded courtyard, with the increasing heat of the day radiating off its marble surface. In the corner, I spotted the café which if I hadn't been told otherwise, I would've assumed was closed. But Emil pushed open the door to reveal—to my surprise—the early stages of a hipster café. I say early stages because while it contained a few trappings of a modern cafe—wooden fixtures, jars in place of glasses, and the two baristas both wearing suspenders—that was largely the extent of it, as if the owner had run out of money halfway through. For one thing, the male barista wasn't bearded, though to be fair to him he didn't really have a choice. In 2005 the First President had announced on State Television (aka *all television*) that from henceforth beards were not to be worn for those under 40, at which point it was then to be expected. No explanation had been given. After the First President's death, this rule became a little less enforced though this changed in early 2019 when the rule was 're-launched' with reports of bearded men being yanked off the streets and forced to shave. For an Islamic country, this seemed particularly unusual, though it has been suggested that it is *because* a beard is seen as being a member of an Islamic movement, that it is therefore illegal.

It only dawned on me later that wearing a beard during my time in Turkmenistan must've been seen as somewhat subversive. Sadly, drinking a hot coffee in the hot sun, with no one about, wasn't as fun as it sounded so we walked back to the car slightly dejected.

*   *   *   *

Much like the day earlier, we spent this one moving between monuments, a routine similar to that I had taken years earlier when I visited North Korea. One of many similarities between the two countries. Both were closed societies of oppressed people living in a version of Utopia, both were overseen by an omnipotent and omnipresent iron fisted dictator. There were also differences, the primary one being that Turkmenistan had money, but the other being the people. While there was no chance of interacting with North Koreans, while driving through the streets of Pyongyang you at least saw them. In this instance, it seemed those people didn't exist. And it was all rather sad. I felt for my guide, a 28-year-old woman exposed to the outside world through her line of work yet more or less trapped in a world not of her own making.

As the day drew to a close, and after having visited polished statues, walked through green luscious but empty parks, and finally having wandered through the 'Russian bazaar' where old ladies sat behind unsold produce, I returned to my hotel.

"Is there anything you'd like to do tonight?" Asked Emil. "Yes actually, I'd like to go to a bar". She thought for a moment and responded that yes, she knew one nearby.

Great, I thought and after being dropped back at my hotel, I jumped in the shower in a giddy state of excitement, ironed a shirt and put on a liberal amount of cologne, heading to the hotel bar to wait for my ride. And, at 7.30 pm on the dot, my government appointed guide and driver picked me up for a night out in Ashgabat and took me to 'The City Pub'.

Now, you could smoke at this pub, which of course was a good thing. But that's where it ended. The television in the corner playing loud hyper-sexualised Russian pop music provided the pub with an atmosphere of sophistication, while the wooden bar and stools justified the 'pub' part of the name, though in contradiction to a TripAdvisor review of "not really a pub". To be fair to Emil, from the way in which she drank her beer, primarily by staring at it, she wasn't much of a drinker. And since the google reviews for this place gave it 4.6/5, I imagine she rightly consulted Google which sent her here. Though this wasn't exactly the fun experience I had envisaged and after consuming enough alcohol and cigarettes to kill a tribe of Turkmen guides, we shifted to a nearby open-air restaurant.

"No, I am sorry sir, we don't have that either tonight", said the waiter for the third time as I continued to request things they didn't have. The menu was a shambles. Most of the items I wanted they didn't have, and the prices were all over the place with the menu marked up with new prices on top of white-out on top of the old prices. You see, the Turkmen currency was currently undergoing rapid rates of inflation, not Venezuela or Zimbabwe levels (yet), but rising so quickly that stores, rather than taking down prices were simply overlaying last week's prices with this week's prices, and restaurants whiting out last week's prices and rewriting the new prices on top. As is almost always the case, this was a result of economic mismanagement by a government running amok, held back by little in the way of checks and balances. The government had for instance recently embarked on a massive spending spree on things the country didn't need, such as the world's largest indoor Ferris wheel looking over an empty desert plain, $5 billion on the extremely extravagant Asian Indoor and Martial Arts Games with its idle monorail and amongst other things, a state of the art airport that was easily one of the best—and emptiest—airports I had ever been in. And to add salt to the wounds of the people whose money the government had just spent, the government then closed the currency exchange offices to the public. And given that people around the world weren't clambering over themselves to exchange their own money for Turkmenistan Manat, it meant that the Turkmenistan population was essentially trapped in its own country. The immediate effect for me was, that rather than changing my USD for Turkmen Manet in the hotel, Emil would insist on exchanging it with her. She would give me the official exchange rate of 3.50 Turkmen Manet to the US dollar, whereas on the black market it would be worth much more. I was used to being ripped off in Central Asia, but this was the one time I simply didn't mind. My guide was sweet, and despite her insistence on life in Turkmenistan being perfect, it was clear to see that like any other 28-year-old exposed to the modern world, she too yearned for a better and freer life. I could read between the lines for instance that she quite liked the German tourist who had travelled by himself through the country a couple of months earlier, as she feigned shock while recalling his views on politics, sex and life in general. This shock seemed to me to be secret titillation.

"Why don't we walk back to the hotel instead of drive?", I suggested to Emil, which she pondered for a moment, knowing that it would probably be frowned upon by the government, but—perhaps because of the beer—agreed. And so, Emil and I walked home along the pristine but empty streets of Ashgabat, with fountains putting on their shows solely for us, and traffic lights ticking to no one. Absurdly, we couldn't stroll at a leisurely pace because of an 11 pm curfew across Ashgabat. "Why is there a curfew, and why do I have to have a guide with me?" I asked, knowing full well that the true answer was simply 'an insane government'. "It is for your protection actually", explained Emil, "in other countries, if you go for a walk and fall down and hurt yourself, no one is there to help you. And sometimes you just die with no one about. Here, our government looks after you and always makes sure you're safe. And the 11 pm curfew is because nothing good happens late at night anyway", that last sentence sounding an awful lot like the puritanical Sydney local council. But you know what, walking down the pristine tree-lined streets with no car engines racing by, past white marbled buildings with their neat gold trim elegantly lit up, in the balmy air of a summer night and almost hand in hand with my very sweet guide, was actually quite lovely.

# MARY

hrist, I almost liked Ashgabat last night", I thought to myself as I sat in the dining hall of my hotel eating a plate of nuts and dried fruits while nursing a self-inflicted headache. A television was showing the President stepping off his jet and walking commandingly down a line of men in military fatigues. Each man dropped to his knees and sycophantically grabbed and kissed the nonchalantly draped hand of the President as he marched past in clear annoyance. Quite a different image of the President's personality than the ones presented on the billboards I thought. Intriguing as this was to watch, I couldn't stay as I had only a couple of hours before my flight. This would be my last day in Turkmenistan, and I was spending it in the country's third-largest city, Mary, before catching a late flight back to Ashgabat for a 2.25 am departure from this Turkmen's idea of Paradise.

Emil waited for me in the hotel's empty cavernous foyer while I paid my tab with the few remaining Turkmen manet that I had left, the hotel not being able to accept credit card. I said my goodbyes to the reception staff and loaded the car with my baggage, wondering to myself when they'd have their next New Zealander staying.

We arrived at the domestic airport, which compared with the rest of the city was rundown and disorderly, and—astonishingly—filled with people, all chaotically moving amongst each other, dragging what seemed to be their lives in bags held together with string. Queues snaked their way through the crowds, as the few check-in counters struggled to process so many people. If they were all fleeing the city, I could hardly blame them, though it seemed simply that the place was understaffed and under-resourced, presumably all the region's money being spent on the city's marble. Emil had insisted that in this land of paradise without want, that it would be safer that we take my bags for the day trip rather than leave them with the driver, obliging us to go through the slow-motion process of checking my bags in. This at least allowed me an unfettered view of the people, many of whom were wearing their national dress. Old men wandered through the crowds, especially conspicuous by their long colourful coats and luxurious beards worn á la Amish. The women wore long—strangely body-hugging—bright green and red dresses, embroidered with ostentatious displays of jewellery. That they were all rather pretty made the scene all the more striking. It was actually a point noted years earlier by Alexander Burns as he passed through the region in 1831 "…in no part of the world have I seen a more rude and healthy race of damsels…" and presumably Alexander the Great, who took his wife Roxanna from the area—"the most beautiful lady in all Asia".*

An hour or so later, Emil and I were stepping off our plane and walking along the tarmac of the Mary "International" Airport. 'International' being a slight misnomer and not in fact reflecting passenger planes from across the globe circling above us, waiting patiently in line to land and deposit their international passengers, but due to the twice a week cargo-only flight to Tbilisi. Greeting us on the tarmac was a large smiling photo of the President, crudely photoshopped into the foreground of the Turkmen flag, and greeting us outside of the airport was our new driver for our day in Mary.

\*    \*    \*    \*

Built in 1884 by the Russian Empire soon after building Ashgabat, and now home to 123,000 Turkmen, Mary has come to be the industrial engine for the country, being the centre for gas and cotton, its two major exports. While it contained the occasional gleaming white marble government building, and indeed even a golden statue to the First President, these were anomalies in an otherwise desert city with streets filled with cars, and the pavements with people. It seemed rather absurd that the country's wealth was being

---

*    *Alexander the Great,* Robin Lane Fox

spent in a city with an invisible population, instead of here where people actually appeared to exist, and in a city where a couple of coats of paint wouldn't have gone astray. But what must surely be a Turkmen saying, "His Excellency, Arkadag*, President Gurbanguly Berdimuhamedov works in mysterious ways". The primary reason for my travel here, however, was not to visit Mary but rather the ruins of an adjacent city that for much of its history was known as 'Queen of the World', the ancient city of Merv.

*        *        *        *

Since almost its founding as an early ancient Persian city, Merv held its status as one of the great cities of the world. It was long regarded as the 'gates to Central Asia' and acted as the staging post for Arab invaders who used it as their base while launching attacks on Central Asian cities further north. Greek fortifications stand as testament to its position as a major city in the Empire left behind by Alexander the Great many centuries earlier, and for a while, it took its name. Buddhist monasteries and artefacts strewn throughout the ruins reflected the city as the westernmost point of Buddhism's spread from Asia, and Zoroastrian tradition mentioned the city as one of the sixteen lands** created by Ahura Mazda***. A clever network of major dams and canals

---

\*      The title the President bestowed upon himself meaning 'The Patron'
\*\*     See Religious Landscape of the Ancient Merv Oasis
\*\*\*The creator and highest deity in Zoroastranism.

were built over the centuries that maintained a water supply to the growing city year-round, all overseen by the mir-ab* of the city who was said to have over 10,000 people under his command. Food was able to be kept in specially designed and insulated dome-shaped brick houses, that were stocked with ice in winter and kept food refrigerated through the harsh desert summer. Numerous madrassahs educated the population while mausoleums were continually built honouring the ever-changing leadership in the region. All of which was divided by inner city walls and citadels into different cities within a city. And defending this enormous oasis city were the kilometres of outer walls, some up to 20 m high, providing a seemingly impenetrable barrier. All to protect a population, that by the 12th century had grown to 700,000 people and a city that had grown into the world's richest. Yet this was sadly to become its historical high point. And when refugees started streaming through the heavily fortified gates of the city in 1221, it acted as a forewarning that everything was about to change.

Led by Genghis's son Tolui, a son who *Genghis* had referred to as 'hot-headed', the Mongol army arrived soon after the refugees and proceeded to place the city under siege. The city held out for seven days until its leadership, having heard reports of what had happened to resisting cities to the north, gave in and surrendered. Whatever the terms of the

---

* Water Bailiff. https://www.theguardian.com/cities/2016/aug/12/lost-cities-merv-worlds-biggest-city-razed-turkmenistan

surrender, they surely did not include the complete massacre of the city and its inhabitants, with each Mongol being ordered to bring back three Merv heads. Compared with the bombing of Hiroshima which saw the deaths of 170,000 people, it is not hard to understand why the massacre of what some historians say was up to 1.2 million people, is regarded to this day as *the* bloodiest capture of a city in history.

While the city attempted to rebuild itself following this onslaught, it never regained its prominence and by the time the Russians began appearing in the 19th century, had simply become a backwater, containing the detritus of a long since gone civilisation. However, it did not disappear into obscurity, for it was seen as one more steppingstone for the Russian's presumed march towards India. Indeed, it was often discussed in the alarmist British Press, which in turn was ridiculed as 'merv-ousness'. But following the Russian's establishment of Mary next door, its fate as a pile of ruins was sealed. "Very decrepit and sorrowful looked those wasting walls of sun-dried clay, these broken arches and tottering towers", described George Curzon, the future Viceroy of India, on his arrival there in 1888.

*    *    *    *

Emil and I wandered amongst the heavily eroded mud and stone architecture sitting amongst a rough terrain of sand and shrubs. We approached the mud walls that had formed the outer barrier of the city, and the fortress known as Erk-Kala that was unable to withstand the ferociousness of Genghis

Khan those 800 years earlier. "Climb up this wall and you'll be able to enter the fortress, I can't join you because I'm too fat", which isn't exactly what Emil said—it actually included "… because of the snakes", but I was reading between the lines. Avoiding zero snakes, I climbed up the 30 m wall and into the Erk-Kala which resembled more of a crater than a citadel. At 20 hectares this fortress was big and while eroded by time, you could still make out the tower structures that had formed part of its defence. The ground was covered in broken ancient pottery that crunched under my feet and which was hard not to imagine was a consequence of the wanton destruction laid down on this city all those years ago. I walked out along the top of one of the walls and looked out across what was once Merv, catching in the distance the rather beautiful Great Kyz Kala, or "Maidens Castle". It has been suggested that this had acted as a girl's madrassah, and it is said that this was where 40 girls threw themselves to their death to avoid the atrocities that would undoubtedly be inflicted upon them by the Mongols streaming in the streets below.

I slid back down the side of the mud wall and jumped in the car to drive across the broken landscape to the Sultan Sanjar Mausoleum, a tomb that had been sitting here in the desert since 1157. It had once sat adjacent to a mosque, all amongst gardens, but these were razed to the ground by the Mongols as they destroyed the city. The tomb was greatly damaged but avoided complete destruction, and sat in ruins for almost 800 years until the Turkish Government paid for its restoration in the 1990s. It's an important monument to the country, appearing on Turkmen money, and acts as a site of pilgrimage for travelling Sufi's. Twenty of whom had just visited, and were just sitting down to lunch nearby when they spotted me. "Something something something", they shouted to me, which Emil explained as them wanting me to join them.

I wandered over, a little trepidatious as twenty pilgrims stared almost in disbelief, the men sitting cross-legged on a raised platform, and their children and wives to the side, all eyes fixed on me. They motioned for me to join them on the platform, and after removing my shoes, I stepped up and sat down with them. The toothless patriarch peppered me with questions, which Emil translated from a little distance, not being able to join the male-only table. For a country receiving 8,000 tourists a year, occupied by people wearing clothes that hadn't changed in a few hundred years, a hipster-looking man bun wearing New Zealander was very much a novelty. Each answer Emil translated back to them was met with warm murmuring, though I could tell they were a little confused when I explained where I was from. They implored me to share with them the dish that was placed between us, a large steel bowl of muddy water with nondescript floating pieces of meat all covered in a good number of flies. I could hardly say no and certainly didn't as the patriarch picked up a big circle of bread, tore it apart with his dirt-covered hands, and handed it to me, motioning me to use it as a spoon. With everyone silently watching, I dipped the bread into the bowl—the flies all launching into the air—and scooped up some of the liquid and meat. If anything, I thought, this would at least act as a laxative, and really it wasn't that bad— (very) fatty lamb meat in a watery broth*. *More!* They insisted and so not wishing to offend, I went back in for seconds and then thirds before I'd finished my bread. "Say xyz to them", Emil quietly whispered to me, which after doing so caused them all to solemnly bow their heads in a warm gesture. I thanked them in English and mistakenly offered them an Indian namaste bow, before stepping down from the platform. Two small children ran up to me and in an attempt at being playful, I overdid a monster impression forcing them both to scream out loud and break into tears, bringing the entire experience to an awkward close.

We took a circuitous route out of Merv and back to Mary, stopping briefly by some of the crumbling brick tombs that had once served as coolhouses. But for an inconspicuous and weather-worn plaque, nothing else marked the site of any significance. It was like much else across this vast destroyed city, an ancient city that had been home to millions of people across time, that now sat eroding and falling to the wayside under a corrupt and indifferent government.

\*　\*　\*　\*

There was one final thing that Emil had wanted to show me in Mary, and sadly that was the National History and

---

\* Covered in flies.

Ethnology Museum. Had we been in another city, say…
Paris, then I would have skipped this, but being in Mary
with no internet offering any diversion and no ATM offering
any money, I didn't really have a choice but to kill an hour.

We approached the white marble building, paid our entrance fee and made our way around. Many of the lights
had been turned off as had the air-con, presumably to save
on power and possibly in acknowledgement of the lack of
any demand.

Depressingly walking past exhibitions showing what life
*was* like, though indistinguishable from my recent experience with the pilgrims. The clothing was hardly any different, and the fake donkeys were just as real as the ones passing on the street. What made the museum worthwhile in
my view though, was the exhibition dedicated solely to the
current President. Occupying the whole first floor and being the only well-lit area of the museum, the President was
shown in various photos doing unlikely and extraordinary
things. Flying a helicopter, speaking at the United Nations
and always—*always*—smiling. "Hang on a minute, look at
what he's wearing here", I said to Emil as we both peered at
a photo of the President surrounded by perhaps a hundred
military personnel. "Now look over here, he's wearing the
exact same thing", I said as I dragged Emil back to the previous photo. "No, he's not", came the quick reply. But he was,
and he wasn't just wearing the exact same thing, it was the
exact same photo of him as he'd been crudely photoshopped
into each picture. The absurdity of it struck me as somewhat

sad, as if the government was holding up four fingers while insisting, they were five.

*     *     *     *

We returned to Ashgabat at night, with plenty of time before my flight out of the country at 2.55 am. Emil suggested a building from which we could catch a night-time view of the city, but frankly, I was ready to leave this country and carry on with my trip. The absurdity of this Truman-show like city and the disgust in the government oppression was wearing me down. I felt for Emil and I felt for the people, and I also felt for my stomach which had been holding everyone back at school until—following my lunch with the pilgrims—decided the entire school, teachers included, were to be dismissed at once. Not wanting everyone to dangerously spill out onto the streets, I insisted to Emil that we head directly to the international airport.

Our driver shot us back onto the clean and sterile empty roads, driving us past the illuminated fountains, past the golden statues bathed in spotlights, and the gold-trimmed marble buildings all lacking any indication of inhabitation. The newly built international airport came into view, a rather extraordinary building designed to look like an eagle. A huge stylised eagle's head sat at the centre with the large glass frontage cleverly illuminated to depict the slow flapping of its wings. The entire airport had only been finished in 2016, had cost USD$2.3 billion and had the capacity to service 14 million passengers a year, which seemed a little optimistic.

We drove up the ramp towards the departure's terminal, passing one last enormous Las Vegas like fountain. "What do you think Chris, what do you think of Ashgabat?" Emil pleadingly asked me. "It's extraordinary", I replied sincerely which I thought was a diplomatic version of "extraordinarily fucked up". "Ah, I'm so glad you like it", Emil replied. The car pulled up to the entrance, I said goodbye to the driver and jumped out with my bags along with Emil who had insisted that she'd accompany me into the airport. Which was very sweet, but also rather frustrating as the only thing on my mind at this point was finding a bathroom.

We passed through security, three loutish security guards conspicuously laughing amongst themselves as they stared at me. I felt like turning to them, putting my hands in the air and bringing their attention to them and their country and laughing back, but I had no time to waste. "I'll wait with you for a bit if you like", "Ah, it's ok, I'll be ok, you go, I'll stay, you go, thank you, thank you", I stammered out. We hugged, kissed each other on the cheek and as soon as she'd turned, I bolted. Well, I shuffled, but at pace making it just in time to a feeling of such relief that I could only describe as transcendent. My flight didn't depart for another five hours, and being only one of four flights to leave the 'International Airport' that day, the customs hadn't yet opened, meaning I had plenty of time to sit on this throne of mine and ponder. I wondered about my guide, who was roughly my age, was going back into Ashgabat that night to her home, within this jail of a country. I had had a personal connection with her, yet here I was, another outsider who had exited the country as quickly as he'd entered, flush with foreign currency and free ideas, both of which could land her in jail.

It was now almost midnight, I was exhausted, there were no newspapers to buy, I had already lapped the airport three times and finished the one podcast that I had had the foresight to have downloaded. The gates finally opened, and I, along with a smattering of others including a young national Turkmenistan sports team, made our way through to the terminal. With still two hours to spare and no books or newspaper to read or podcast to listen to, I decided to simply lap the terminals and see what I could find. With the ability to handle 14 million passengers a year, the terminal was big. I walked the length of the empty airport passing the military guards who were stationed at various points along the way, all eying me suspiciously. The first approached—"you fly to Turkey?" he barked at me. I nodded, "Back that way", he pointed back down from where I had come. I ignored him and continued walking. A younger friendlier guard approached me and in very broken English explained that I could smoke a cigarette in the bathroom if I so wished. I misinterpreted him and thought he was asking for cigarettes, and happy to oblige, I smiled, nodded and opened my pack to him motioning him to take. His eyes widened, he furtively looked over his shoulder, then shuffled me to the corner. "Yes. Please", he pleaded with me. I gave him five cigarettes, which he took eagerly, bowing with his hand on his heart. I carried on, further down this empty airport until I came across a glass box with 'WIFI' emblazoned across the top. Good God I thought, I couldn't believe my luck. I stepped into the glass box which had four ancient computers lined across one wall and a single attendant in the centre. This was all the luckier, as the flight was delayed by an hour, and we were now leaving at the very punishing hour of 4 am. I downloaded my emails, some news of the outside world and a podcast and made my way back to the gate to finally board my Turkish Airlines flight out of the country.

Landing into Istanbul a few hours later, a tired plane of passengers rose to disembark. A member of the Turkmen sports team rose first, and with a face full of panic and eyes almost in tears, shoved and elbowed his way to the bathroom, causing much consternation from the other passengers. Strange, I thought, I hadn't seen him with us at lunch.

# KYRGYSTAN

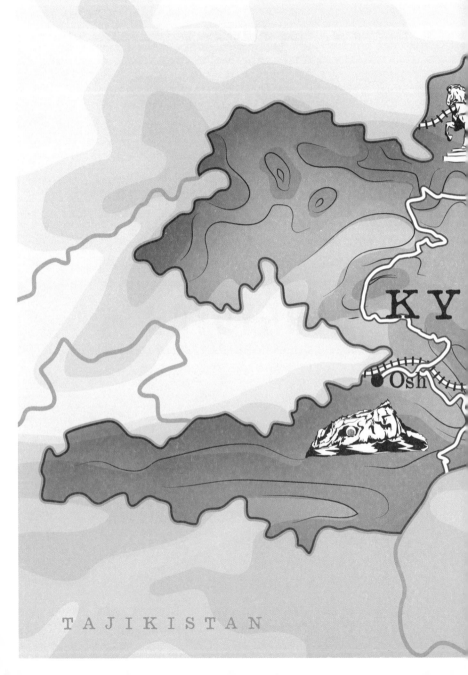

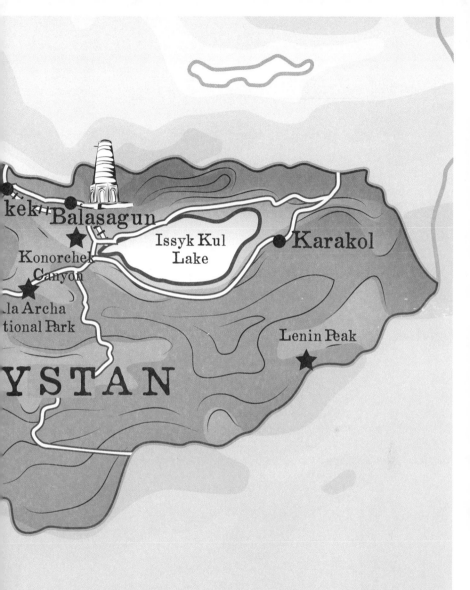

kek

**Balasagun**

Konorchek
Canyon

Issyk Kul
Lake

●Karakol

la Archa
tional Park

Lenin Peak

**YSTAN**

CHINA

edged tightly between Kazakhstan, Tajikistan and China, with the Tien Shan mountain range covering 80% of its landmass and sitting at an average height of 2,750 m above sea level, this country has been described by some as the "Switzerland of Central Asia". Though with no chocolate and less money the comparisons with Switzerland end quickly and once you ignore the geography, disappear altogether. For unlike Switzerland, which among other things has had some sort of defined identity for at least a few hundred years, the Kyrgyz have not. Prior to the Bolsheviks arriving at the start of the 20th century, along with their five-year plans and ideas of nation-building, the landscape had been ruled by everyone in the region *but* the Kyrgyz. It had been part of the Uyghur Empire, the Mongol Empire, and then, of course, Tamerlane's, though with the collapse of his became part of the Uzbeks. This meant for most of the history the Kirghiz, much like the Jews and the Kurds, have been stateless, in turn making them all the more difficult to define. With round faces, narrow eyes and a pale complexion, the Kyrgyz look quite different from their Persian looking Tajik neighbours to their south, though quite similar to the Kazakhs at their north. Indeed, just so as to confuse any aspiring authors, the term Kirghiz throughout historical literature would often be synonymous with Kazakh, with many travellers confusing them as simply another Kazakh tribe. Not hard to do when they look the same, speak in similar languages and both live nomadic lifestyles. But that is not to say there aren't defining features.

For one, the men wear Kalpaks. A tall white felt hat that is worn solely by Kirghiz men and has been for time immortal. Well, at least since 1402 when Tamerlane's armies sieged and kicked out the crusader Knights from Smyrna in modern-day Western Turkey. For the battle was captured in a small Persian painting and clearly shows four rock wielding Kalpak-wearing men. But perhaps the strongest symbol of national identity rests with the Epic of Manas, which at twenty times the length of Homer's Odyssey and Iliad combined, is regarded as the longest epic poem in history[*]. It is said—within Kyrgyzstan—that the Epic retells the story of the Kirghiz, all their myths, tales and legends, going back a thousand years to the 10th century[**] when they united under

---

[*] The Tibetan Epic of King Gesar and the Sanskrit Epic of Mahabharata both have more words, though less verses.

[**] In 1995 the country held nationwide celebrations, celebrating a thousand years of Manas implying a start date for the Epic of 995 AD.

the leadership of a figure named Manas. He is such an important symbol to the nation that his name, his image and his mausoleum appear on banknotes, statues of him appear throughout the country, a 4,500 m high mountain is named after him, as is an asteroid discovered by a Soviet scientist in 1979. That in the early telling of this poem Manas was regarded as the leader of only *one* of the 40 Kirghiz tribes, and that it has been called by one historian as an "absurd gallimaufry of pseudo-history" no longer matters. And nor should it necessarily; a country's traditions and legends are often steeped less in fact, and more in symbolism aimed to idealize positive traits of the people. It does matter however when those traditions serve to perpetuate the suffering of its inhabitants, as with another distinctive Kirgiz feature.

To be entirely fair to the Kirghiz, the practise of bride kidnapping *is* illegal in the country, though this hasn't stopped an estimated 12,000 women a year being literally kidnapped off the street and forced into a marriage by her 'groom'. The Kirgiz term for this 'tradition' is *ala kachuu* which literally means 'grab and run', and involves the 'groom' and his male friends driving up to his target wife on the street, bundling her into the car before speeding off to an ad hoc wedding ceremony. *Sometimes* this is planned. The 'groom' and 'bride' may, in fact, be dating, with the woman expecting that at some point she will be 'grabbed'. By doing this the couple can avoid the high cost of putting on a more normal wedding, which can sometimes run for up to a month and is expected to be paid for by the family of the groom. Often though, the 'bride' in the situation has no relationship with the 'groom' and will unwittingly be snatched straight off the street and driven sometimes hundreds of kilometres into a rural village, fighting and screaming the entire way. On arrival to the groom's family, she will be handed over to the women of the family, themselves often victims of *ala kachuu* where they will spend sometimes days trying to psychologically break down the woman into accepting the marriage. Should the woman refuse the offer of marriage, she will be returned to the street where she was taken from. Though in a country where virginity is regarded as sacrosanct, the mere *suggestion* that she may have slept with the man means that she will be shrouded in shame, with the honour of her and her family violated. Which is why most women will, in fact, accept the marriage, though not all, and instead some will turn to suicide. There was international outrage in 2018 when a 20-year-old medical student was snatched off the streets by a 30-year-old she barely knew in an attempt at marriage. When she managed to phone the police, they arrived placing them both in the same cell where he then stabbed her to death.

The reasoning given by those involved is that this is their tradition and the way of life that they have been practising for millennia. Though like the Epic of Manas, many historians regard this as a bastardisation of the truth. Certainly, courtship by the Kirgiz has historically involved an aggressive display of masculinity. When travelling through the region in 1875, British Colonel Fredrick Burnaby noted that at large public events, Kirgiz women would often mount the fastest horse and race across a field, pursued by men on their own horses. The first to reach her and grab her breast would then have the chance of pursuing a marriage with her. But even *in this instance,* the woman would have a choice.

But speaking of choice, there is one further distinction where Kyrgyzstan differs from its Central Asian neighbours. And that is, it is the *only* county to be run by a democratically elected government. For unlike the other 'stans, their first president wasn't simply the man in control when the Soviet Union collapsed, but instead came to power—God forbid—by a vote from the people. And unlike the dictators surrounding him, he recognised the direction of history and began almost immediately introducing market reforms across the country. "I believe that the revolution in the sphere of economics was not made by Karl Marx but by Adam Smith", he said. Of course, as per the old adage, power corrupts and absolute power corrupts absolutely, and he soon came to quite like his new-found powers and each subsequent election saw both the increase in irregularities with the coincidental increase in voter turnout and approval. That was until 2005 when, following his fourth election win, the country erupted into what became known as the Tulip Revolution, leading to his resignation a month later. Today, amongst a sea of countries regarded by the NGO Freedom House as 'Not Free', Kyrgyzstan sits alone with its 'partly free' status. Something I mentioned to the passenger sitting next to me on the plane, to which she replied, "…yes that's right, here we can tell our government to fuck off".

# BISHKEK

t was 5.35 am when my flight from Istanbul landed into Bishkek's Airport—the Manas International Airport, named after the symbolic mythical figure of the country, which would be the equivalent of naming Athens airport the International Airport of Zeus. Built in Soviet times, the airport was equipped with 4 km long runways, perfect for the large Soviet bombers and military cargo planes that would land here. This also made it perfect for the modern American ones which began landing as America's war in Afghanistan got underway. In fact, this airport became the main entry and exit point for literally millions of military servicemen from 26 different countries that fought in that war. That ended in 2014, when the Kyrgyz government cancelled the agreement following pressure from Russia, unhappy at having the Americans in their backyard.

\*　　\*　　\*　　\*

I waited for my bags and looked through tired eyes around me at the sea of round faces topped with jet black hair, a few Kalpek bobbing amongst them. My battered and looking to burst duffel bag appeared on the turnstile. I lifted with a heave and walked out into the brisk morning, anticipating a rush of drivers though unlike in every other Central Asian port I'd been so far, this one was rather empty. It was of course early morning, but things felt instantly different.

I picked my man who offered to take me into town for a very reasonable USD$5 which I agreed to before jumping into his car. Through his broken English and Google Translate, which he studiously typed away against the wheel while we sped down the highway, he told me that he was a couple of years younger than me and had three kids. "You have kids?" he asked, before looking at me rather suspect when I said no. *Hmmm,* I thought, *I wonder whether this man bun makes me look gay.*

It was so early in the morning that the roads to the hotel had been empty, which, combined with the red lights that Kuba was happy to ignore, meant that I arrived to my hotel a prompt half-hour after exiting the airport. Given this was my first taxi trip which hadn't involved the customary fleecing, I happily tipped Kuba and accepted his offer of being my Bishkek driver for the next few days.

\*　　\*　　\*　　\*

Having crashed into bed on arrival, I woke a few hours later and pulled the curtains to reveal Bishkek in daylight. Between a vast mountain range sat off in the distance and me were dark green tree-lined streets. That Bishkek was known as the greenest city in Central Asia came as no surprise. When it came to the buildings, however, they were much like any other town built by the Soviets—grey, concrete and practical, and on the outskirts tall chimney stacks muddying the sky with their exhaust. The temperature was a nippy 10 degrees—so donning a heavy jacket, I went searching for breakfast.

I wandered along the tree-lined streets, stepping over the deep channels between the pavements rushing with clear alpine water. Like Almaty 100 km to its West, heavy bronze and stone statues sat amongst the trees dedicated to Soviet themes and characters. At one end of a rather lovely boulevard sat the statue of a man astride a horse—sadly not wearing the Kalpek but instead a Budenovka—the hat worn by the Red Army during the Russian civil war. This was Mikhail Frunze, born in what would become Bishkek in 1885, to two Russian parents. Given the area had only been incorporated into Imperial Russia nine years early, his parents had presumably been pioneering settlers. He grew up in pre-Bishkek before being accepted in 1904 to St. Petersburg Polytechnic University, whereby he fell into a group that set his and Russia's future course in motion. That group was the burgeoning communist movement, and when a year later the 1905 revolution broke out, he became the leader in a number of labour movements on strike. When the first revolution simmered down, he was arrested and sentenced to death, though this was reduced and instead he was sent to Siberia. Closer to home which was a plus but sentenced to life hard labour, which was not. Ten years later though he escaped and presumably rather bitter joined the Red Army where he successfully defeated the White Army in numerous battles across the collapsing empire, growing in rank until by 1920 he was the leader of the Red Army in Turkestan. In fact, it was under his leadership that the Red Army smashed the Emir of Bukhara's forces further south, thereby ending half a millennium of Emir rule. From here his profile rose rapidly, evidenced by the paintings of him and Lenin discussing military strategy and grainy photos of him alongside Trostky inspecting Red Army military parades. Like many who shared the company of Stalin in the 1920s though his death was premature, and he died at age 40 in 1925 with his remains being placed in the walls of the Kremlin. In honour of him, the city of Bishkek was renamed after him as the city of Frunze and remained that way until Kyrgyz independence in 1991.

It was hard not to wonder what the modern Kyrgyz thought about these Soviet-era statues. They were very much a part of the Kyrgyz history but represented a complicated portion of it. Certainly, the country was built on the back of Soviet soldiers paid for with Soviet wealth. And indeed, the train station that the Frunze statue faced was built by the Soviets in 1936 and was partly responsible for injecting modernity into this previously primitive part of the world. But it also brought the trains that would take many to their death in World War 2, and more to a lifetime of servitude in a gulag on some distant frozen expanse. While many of the 'woke' concepts sweeping across the Western world would be laughed at here, it wasn't hard to see at least like the confederacy statues in America or the Rhodes statues in Africa, that one day these Soviet statues too would be toppled in a fit against the past.

# IN SEARCH OF A
# WATERFALL

awoke that morning and looked out across to the mountain range on Bishkek's edge that in a few hours I was to hike. My phone showed a message from Kuba informing me that "something has happened, but my brother take you [sic] instead". I showered and wandered downstairs to the lobby where a man giant was sitting waiting for me. He didn't speak a lick of English but through the help of the hotel receptionist, it was determined that this man, who was three times the size of Kuba and had about 20 years on him, was—I was told—the brother of Kuba. I wondered whether by 'brother' he had meant 'comrade' for there was no way he and this guy shared a parent. With a big grin and a bigger handshake however, he greeted me with a 'good morning' the only English words he knew before offering me a cigarette as we jumped into his car.

We headed south out of the city on a long straight road to the Ala Archa National Park. I had done only a little research the night before, but had some understanding that there were a number of trails running throughout the Park, one of which was said to be particularly spectacular and took the hiker to the base of a skyscraper tall waterfall. I couldn't confirm this with my driver as he didn't speak English and, in any case, was content listening to aggressive Russian pop music while being seemingly oblivious to me.

The houses and buildings of Bishkek soon gave way to fields, before in turn giving way to forests as the road continued to steadily climb, with the mountains now looming above us. The road ended eventually at an empty car park. Jumping out and slipping on my small backpack I noted how much colder the air was up here. My driver pointed to the start of a track which sat next to a big board written in a mix of Cyrillic and English, indicating that the waterfall was 2.2 hours of walking and 465 m higher than where I stood. All of which seemed reasonable. I'd hiked in many places around the world, and knew that these boards would always overestimate the time to be safe. In my experience I would often complete the hikes in half the time estimated, which meant in this instance I should be back in at most three hours.

*   *   *   *

"Where is this bloody waterfall?" I muttered to myself as I looked down at my watch two hours later. The walk despite being so far waterfall-less, was indeed spectacular. It had taken me up the angled side of a mountain that fell away to a confluence of valleys below. And in part of these valleys sat a layer of cloud, illuminated by streaks of sunlight from the morning sun that was by now peaking over and through the mountains. And from where the clouds trailed off, I could see the turquoise-blue alpine river against a grey shingled riverbed that was providing a calming white noise backdrop. The vegetation around me had steadily reduced to the point that I was now walking amongst hardy alpine shrubs and a few scattered conifers.

I continued walking, the trail had long since gone and I eventually reached a craggy incline that forced me at some points to climb on all fours. The vegetation now disappeared and instead of hardened earth, the ground was made up of dangerous rock debris. I'd clearly climbed to a reasonable height as snow and ice now began appearing. This was getting silly I thought before concluding *stuff the waterfall*, and began gingerly making my way back down.

It was easier though slightly more precarious on the way back, and it did cross my mind more than once that perhaps these conditions, with no humans around, was the perfect breakfast spot for a bear or pack of wolves. Four hours after I'd set out however, I made it back to the car park just as a single Frenchman was getting himself ready to head up the mountain. "Hi mate", "Bonjour" the bearded man said. "If you're looking for the waterfall, I could not find it. I went right up to the snow line!" "Waterfall?" He said, looking at me quizzically, "…that only runs in Spring".

# OSH

woke at 5.30 am, it was still dark outside. Kuba was arriving at 6.15 am to take me to the airport for my flight to Osh, the second largest and also oldest city of Kyrgyzstan. Having had a fair bit of experience in Central Asian airports by now, I had stressed to Kuba that time was of the essence. He obviously agreed as he was outside by 6.10 am, his multi decade-old BMW softly vibrating from an untuned engine, with fumes visibly coughing from the tailpipe into the brisk morning air. I jumped into the car and greeted the laconic Kuba who gave a quick nod of the head with a cigarette hanging out of his mouth. He put the car into drive, and we shot off through the empty fog-covered streets.

"Car needs petrol", Zuba said as he pointed out a petrol station, "ok, but be quick". He nodded, rolled the car up to the pump, jumped out and with the car still going ran inside to prepay for the petrol, before running back, sparking another cigarette and then proceeding to fill the still running car. Ingeniously efficient I thought.

Avoiding a catastrophic petrol station incident, I arrived at the airport half an hour later, and despite the scrum that had formed around the check in, was able to make it just in time for boarding. The usual motley crew of large families, white kalpaks bobbing along the sea of old Kyrgyz men heads, many quietly staring at me, and together we walked across the tarmac to our plane, the morning light diffusing through the fog.

The plane rose through the mixture of fog and smog that blanketed the city, and after reaching a sufficient height gave me a glorious view over the Tien Shan mountains below and the Ala Archa National Park that I'd been hiking the previous day. This forty-minute flight took us over a beautiful array of snow-capped mountain peaks, dramatically dissected by rivers, and covered in thick carpets of forest. Slowly this gave way to the Ferghana Valley, a flat plain encircled almost entirely by mountains and with towns and farmland spread across it. It was such a fertile part of Central Asia, that it is often referred to as the region's 'breadbasket' and is home to a quarter of the region's population. And sitting on this plain, nestled against the surrounding mountains came into view a city whose name in Uzbek meant 'Pilov', the city of Osh.

*    *    *    *

Referred to as Kyrgyzstan's 'capital of the south', Osh has been standing here for 3,000 years and had been controlled by the Uzbeks for a few 100 years before Stalin appeared with his map and pen. Which meant that despite a large portion of its population being Uzbek it is actually controlled by Kyrgyzstan, a point of contention which had simmered below the surface since the breakup of the Soviet Union, until finally erupting in ethnic rioting in 2010. The rioting only lasted a few days before being put down by the Kyrgyz security forces, but saw the deaths of 893 and the creation of between 100,000-250,000 Uzbeki refugees.

While the circumstances were entirely different, this wasn't the first time there had been a rebellion here against an Uzbeki population. Half a millennium earlier, as the remnants of Tamerlane's empire were being fought over, a descendant of Tamerlane named Babur established himself in Osh. And as the Uzbeks swept down from the north, capturing pieces of Tamerlane's decaying empire, they came into direct conflict with him. Over the course of almost two decades, the fortunes of Babur rose and fell, with the control of Osh, Samarkand and the Ferghana valley swapping three times between him and these new Uzbeks. Ultimately, Babur would lose and left with his army southward and into the Indian sub-continent. There he was successful and established the Mughal Empire, which would eventually become one of the largest and wealthiest empires in history, and produce monuments such as the Agra Fort and Taj Mahal. Sadly, he didn't leave behind any Taj Mahal equivalents in Osh, though he did leave behind a small mosque sitting atop Sulyman Mountain.

You see Sulyman Mountain almost immediately upon entering Osh as its steep craggy sides rise from the city's centre and dominate the skyline. It is such a conspicuous landmark that during the age of the Silk Road it was regarded as the halfway mark, being referred to in numerous historical accounts of the region, and—some would argue—being mentioned by the Greco-Roman geographer Ptolemy in the 2nd century AD*. And having checked into my hotel, it was here where I headed first.

\*   \*   \*   \*

I made my way through the streets of Osh, moving broadly in the direction of the mountain until I reached a gate at its base that marked the entrance to pathways running up its side. High up above me stood a large glass and steel retro Soviet structure, that had been built in 1978 by the Soviets to mark 3,000 years of human occupation of Osh. I followed a dirt track until I reached its entrance, and paying a small fee entered through a door and into the start of a cave system that turned out to be a museum. Inside was a warren of different coves, each containing a diorama displaying different peoples who once occupied this land. Apart from the *two* ladies behind the counter—which seemed excessive—the cave system and museum were empty. I worked my way around the strange displays, conscious that I was being

---

\*   There is debate where exactly along the Silk Road Ptolemy meant when he referred to the Stone Tower.

closely monitored by the staff. The cave system meandered through the mountain, following it until I reached its exit that opened out onto a trail. Following this trail, I reached a platform which sat alongside the mosque built by Babur half a millennium before. Down below me spread Osh surrounded by vast fields of farmland. Spreading west was the Ferghana Valley, and south and east the surrounding mountains that hemmed this valley in. A brown pall of smoke sat in the air above the city but below where I was standing, caused by innumerable household chimneys and presumably the decades-old cars. Through the city ran a river fed by an alpine lake in the surrounding mountains. I had been told to follow the river to the city market where I'd find a good lunch, and given that it was nearing lunchtime and I couldn't find a good reason to use the mosque adjacent to me, I decided that the city market would be where I headed next.

*   *   *   *

I followed the river and entered the market, another of which made the claim to be Central Asia's largest. Throngs of people were shuffling between and negotiating with sellers who were screaming from their stalls. Piles of offal rose high, and heads of goat lay stacked on top of one another, at which point I realised I was no longer hungry. I continued through and came to an ad hoc bar where four rough-looking men stood, knocking back shots of something clear that I doubted was water. For some reason I joined them, took the glass of what they offered me along with one of their cigarettes, knocking back both in quick time. *For God's Sake, why the hell did I do that!* I wondered as the liquid dropped aggressively into my stomach. Without a common language, it was impossible to communicate with the blokes, particularly as they were so drunk, so I thanked them for the cigarette and left.

*God that tasted terrible* I thought as whatever I'd just consumed churned around my stomach. I followed the river back towards my hotel until I arrived at a quiet plaza with what I came to discover was Central Asia's largest statue of Lenin. He stood in front of a government building, his arm outstretched to an imaginary people, the same pose he was depicted as holding in almost every statue of him across the world. I suppose this was on purpose, for he was always more of a symbol than a person. As the head of the Bolsheviks, his relationship with Stalin had grown increasingly fractious, and he had proposed to the party management that Stalin be removed from his position. But after suffering a stroke in 1922, Stalin was able to surreptitiously consolidate power around himself and by doing so, positioned himself as Lenin's confidante and natural successor. When Lenin died prematurely at the age of 53 in 1924, it was then that these statues started appearing. Perhaps not necessarily to invoke a memory of Lenin, but rather to drill into the observers that by building these, Stalin was his natural heir.

\*    \*    \*    \*

I set out that evening in search of a restaurant and stumbled across a rather grand one overlooking the city's river.

It was large with absurdly loud Russian club music playing in the front hall that overlooked the road, but entirely quiet out the back, which overlooked the river and moreover had been designated the smoking section. Pity the non-smokers who had to choose between smoky silence, or deafening fresh air, though I suppose non-smokers didn't yet exist in this country. I chose the smoking section with glee as an attractive waitress came to take my order, eager to try out her English, me eager to let her. Traditionally dressed Kyrgyz families and young couples occupied the tables around me, the men always smoking, the women always demure. I ordered a borsch, a local beer, lit up a cigarette and sat back to my book, *The Day Lasts More Than a Hundred Years* written by Kyrgyzstan's *most* celebrated author, Chingiz Aitmatov.

Born in 1928 into the newly established Kirghiz Soviet Republic[*], Aitmatov would become a celebrated author both inside the Soviet Union and out, winning him numerous global literary prizes. His rocketing fame launched a political career, where he acted as advisor to Mikhail Gorbachev and Soviet ambassador to Luxemburg, before becoming Kyrgyzstan's ambassador to Belgium, Luxemburg and The Netherlands and representative to the European Union, NATO and UNESCO. He was a true believer in communism, which is perhaps unsurprising given how he

---

[*]  Its actual name was the Kirgiz Autonomous Socialist Soviet Republic, a mouthful of a name that had replaced an equally verbose Kara-Kirghiz Autonomous Oblast.

benefited from it. Less so when you consider that his father, himself a true supporter of communism, was arrested during Stalin's 1937 purge, found to be guilty of "bourgeoise nationalism" and executed. This paradox was reflected in the nuance within his writing, where he saw communism's failures not as a product of the system but because of (Soviet) human nature itself. Which reminds me of a Soviet joke...

*Igor and Boris are dirt-poor peasants, barely scratching enough crops from their small plots of land to feed their families. The only difference between them is that Boris owns a scrawny goat. One day a fairy appears to Igor and grants him a wish. Igor says, "I wish that Boris's goat should die".*

\*    \*    \*    \*

A couple of days later, I was departing Osh but not before spending the day in the mountains to the city's south. I'd had breakfast in the hotel that morning, as three men wearing surprisingly sharp suits and their Kalpeks walked in. For some reason they all glared at me while sitting down, but all I could think was *God I love those hats*.

The driver I'd arranged the night before greeted me in the hotel foyer with a broad missing-teeth smile set in a cheerful but weather-worn face, and a firm handshake from a strong coarse hand. My impression was that he must've been in his early 50s and was embarrassingly inconspicuously shocked when he later revealed that he wasn't that much older than me.

My Benjamin Button guide and I jumped into his truck and meandered through the traffic-filled streets of Osh, bumper to bumper with beaten up old cars, before the traffic petered out and we entered the broad empty road that exited the city. We cut through the surrounding landscape, made up of dry pale-yellow undulating hills marked only by rusty streaks and unbridled horses that trotted in the distance. Our road wound its way through these hills which were blocking the horizon, until the road began descending following a wide arc, with the landscape opening and revealing a wall of distant mountains. We were eye level with the foothills of these mountains and were dropping towards their base, while behind them sat rows of mountains with each set rising then dropping then rising even higher like waves. The great distance between us and the mountains shrouded them in haze, presenting them as one massive homogenous barrier. This was the start of the Alay mountain ranges that connected to the Tien Shan mountains in the North West and the Pamir Ranges in the South. While these ranges would reach heights of 5.5 km, sitting just behind them on the border of Kyrgyzstan and Tajikistan sat Lenin Peak (named in Tajikistan as Avicenna Peak after the 10th century Bukharan born mathematician) which sat at over 7 km high. It had originally been named Mount Kaufman after the first Russian Governor-General of Turkestan who had made his name by capturing Khiva in 1873. But when the first set of Russian imperialists were replaced with the second, and thinking that this was the tallest peak in the USSR*, it was named Lenin Peak with a bust of Lenin's head being placed at its peak, where it still sits today.

The mountain range took up more of our windscreen as we descended towards its base. The road we were on entered into small villages, where we passed quaint village scenes with gatherings of men in formal attire and wearing the Kalpek. The sealed road soon gave way to gravel, the villages became less developed with houses replacing apartment blocks and eventually huts replacing the houses. Lone old ladies sat on the side of the road selling fruit and milk. But then even this too passed, and we soon found ourselves on a broken mud track that cut through a valley and into the mountains which were now on top of us. A pristine alpine river flowed adjacent to the track, and we bumpily drove along as green hills raced away from either side of us and up into sharp peaks scraping the sky.

The sun beamed down upon us and despite the snow along the mountain tops, the air remained warm. The river cut through the mountains, and we followed it around where the landscape opened into a wide green Sound-Of-Music looking plain. Small huts dotted the undulating green hills, and amongst them sat sown fields, separated by rows of poplars. Small tufts of clouds hung around the peaks and the river sparkled in the clear bright sunlight.

---

* It was later discovered that Stalin Peak in Tajikistan was the highest, a mountain now known as Ismoil Samoni Peak.

My guide turned the truck up onto a private driveway that led to a small house where he indicated we'd stop for lunch. A woman with mostly missing but otherwise blackened teeth shyly came out to greet us, before leading us through a small gate and into the front yard of her house which overlooked the valley below us. Two small neatly dressed children ran out from the house chasing one another, both abruptly stopping in their tracks when they saw me. They politely shook my hands, not quite being able to look me in the eyes before running away. An extremely old lady who must've been pushing 140, but who I was told was 89, bent almost perpendicular and balancing on a stick, slowly made her way towards me. She grabbed my hands with paper-thin skin, stared up at me beaming from her watery eyes. Smoke rose from the house's chimney before stopping twenty or so minutes later, suggesting lunch was now ready. I was directed into a yurt some way away from the house, crouching down to enter. A thick carpet patterned with geometric shapes covered the floor, while crisscrossing pieces of wood bound in rope and covered in an outer layer of red fabric embraided with Islamic shapes formed the inner walls. The skins of foxes hung from the sides above plush pillows that served as seats. The two boys came in holding trays of food, dumplings, piles of fresh bread and a doughy pie-like dish called Oromo, before bowing and darting back out. My guide and I sat in silence, while we ate this extremely filling food, before washing it down with tea. We finally finished, and I was eager to get walking. I'd planned the entire day around a large hike through the mountains, but had instead spent two hours in a car and over an hour stuffing around in this house. I thanked and tipped the lady, patted the kids on their heads, and told my driver I was going for a walk and would be back soon.

I wandered out from the house and down towards the river, following a small dirt track that led off into the mountains. Small huts sat nestled in the hills above me, but nothing stirred in them, no hidden engine noise wafted down from them, nothing to break the silence but for the river washing down from the mountains. I put on a podcast that was discussing the possibility that supersonic commercial flight would be making a comeback in the next two decades, nicely juxtaposing with the ancient agrarian life that surrounded me.

The track continued up into the hills until I could see it peter out into a clearing surrounded by thick green forest. Two small houses sat amongst the clearing, and behind them, the forests continued up until they reached clear hills that steeply formed into the base of a wall of grey rugged mountains, covered in layers of snow. Two cows appeared on the track and began making their way towards me and unsure of what to do in a cow encounter, I turned and in a not too confident trot made my way back.

I woke my guide who had since fallen asleep and showed him some of the photos I'd taken of where I'd just been, though it was the phone and my wireless air buds that he showed the most interest in. We began our long journey back to the Osh Airport, and with the limited communication between us long since dry, I felt disappointed in myself that I hadn't learnt at least *a little* Russian. My guide made light of things though and had discovered the English word 'girl-friend' which he humorously used while pointing at girls along the roadside, though this became tiresome after the third girl appeared, and exhausting thereafter.

We broke through the mountains and back onto the Ferghana Valley before reaching the airport. As my flight eventually took off, I scanned out across the Valley back towards the mountains I'd just been. They were one part of the ranges that ringed this Valley, feeding it with the water that made it so fertile, allowing its cities to grow, marking them as the unfortunate targets of so much historical ambition.

# SLIPPING THROUGH
# A CANYON

There?" Kuba nodded back. "Where?" "There!" Kuba was pointing at a mound of rocks that he was insisting was the entry point to the Konorchek Canyon, a set of canyons referred to as 'The Grand Canyon of Kyrgyzstan', which I later concluded to be a rather gross misrepresentation.

Clambering up a wall of rocks and then scrambling across a train line, I eventually stumbled across the start of the canyon formation. And as soon as I had disappeared around the first corner, I felt extremely and happily isolated. I checked my phone's map and laughed when I saw where I was, a small blue dot, so isolated from everywhere in the world. Throwing on a podcast, I hiked my way for the next couple of hours, walking amongst the extraordinarily high copper coloured cliffs on either side of me, formed by a long since gone river. Quiet but for my steps and the podcast in my ears, until from nowhere came a low grumble, the noise gradually increasing until it was reverberating amongst the cliffs. *Shit, a flash flood!* … was my first thought, but no… instead, as the sound rose rapidly, a fighter jet screamed low overhead followed quickly by another. The noise ripped through the sky dropping off until it shot back up again as they banked and flew straight back over. In a region littered with US air force bases, all on the edge of Russia, India and China, it was hard not to let the mind wander. But after another two swoops, they were gone, leaving me and my podcast alone.

I continued walking until the canyon opened into a great wide-open V where two rivers must've once converged. It had been three hours since I'd last spoken with Kuba and but for the sudden appearance of the fighter planes, nothing had offered the tiniest distraction. And so, I was given a fright when as if from nowhere I caught sight of what I thought to be a person disappear behind a rock. Which suddenly felt extremely bloody creepy. *Had I just seen a person, and had that person seen me?* I wondered. I determined that I would find them before they found me again and scrambled up the dusty hill that formed at the centre of the V. I made it to the top and scanned the landscape below me and yes, I could see someone. A lone Kyrgyz shepherd with his dog and a grazing flock of sheep. Thinking that a rural Kyrgyz man might be startled by an Australian covered all in black and appearing from nowhere, I stopped and turned back.

I raced back both due to the decline and the fact that I'd been gone for so long, and accidentally took a slightly different return route. About five minutes from where the car was parked, instead of the track that I'd entered on, I came across a dried-up pond, with deep cracks marbled through the hardened mud like you see so often during droughts. I thought if I just hop from one cracked segment to the other, I could make it across and so launched myself from the hardened ground landing thigh-deep in thick mud. Occurring so abruptly, I slightly panicked and shifting my weight sunk a little further. Splaying myself spreadeagled across the top of the mud, I clutched at some plants, pulling myself out of the suction like grip, and shifting my body weight so that I was able to slither across the mud on my stomach, until I reached firm ground.

Kuba had shifted his seat horizontal and was asleep in the driver's seat. I knocked on the window, to which he lazily opened his eyes before bolting upright to stare at me in shock. He jumped out of the car and said a few things in Kyrgyz which sounded like swearing. Then said a few more, before animatedly telling me I couldn't enter the car. Half an hour later, my pile of muddy clothes were in the boot while Kuba and I, now wrapped in a towel, raced home.

*    *    *    *

I was flying out the following day to Dushanbe, capital of Tajikistan. I decided that I'd get up early and find a gym before exploring the city one last time. Jogging down the splendid Erkindik Avenue, with heavy trees lining the pedestrianised centre of this avenue, and past the monument to a Kyrgyz poet, I couldn't help notice that everyone was staring at me. I had become somewhat immune to being stared at over the past few weeks, but this staring was slightly unusual, as if they saw *me* as slightly unusual. And then it dawned on me, I was wearing shorts, and not just shorts, but quite tiny gym shorts revealing my hedonistic western thighs. Kyrgyzstan is a conservative country, and following this strange response I'd elicited I looked online and came across a discussion board where one user had posted *"If you have ¾ pants you will get ¼ less respect from local males than those wearing 1/1 pants"*. Given I was wearing the equivalent of 1/8 pants, then a simple calculation suggested I was receiving 1/2 less respect. Thank god I hadn't run in my speedos.

# TAJIKISTAN

Yep, I would be cautious if I were you", a Tajik bloke I'd met in Kazakhstan had said to me after I'd explained to him my plan. My plan for Tajikistan and Kyrgyzstan had been to start in Dushanbe, Tajikistan's capital, and over the course of two weeks bounce along the Pamir Highway. This would first take me south to the border of Afghanistan, which I would skirt before turning north and up into the Pamir Mountain Range, and then finally drop into the plains of Kyrgyzstan and end in the Kyrgyz city of Osh. Starting at 800 m above sea level and climbing another almost 4000 m, this 1200 km long highway is one of those forgotten feats of human engineering where enormous natural obstacles were overcome by sheer force of will. It was originally conceived at the height of the Great Game when a paranoid Russian Empire perceived an imminent push north by the British from their Indian stronghold and needed the ability to transport troops quickly south. The Soviets, equally concerned by this potential threat, then reinforced it in the 1930s making it more capable for the much larger military machines that would now pass across it and largely making it what it is today. And the reason to drive it?—The chance to cut through extraordinary rugged mountain landscapes, stay overnight in isolated little towns tucked away in the middle of nowhere and to mix with people lost to the modern world. But with this bloke's warning along with multiple others, in particular, my mother's, and arriving only a few months after four cyclists from America, the Netherlands and Switzerland doing a similar trip had been murdered by ISIS, I decided to, unfortunately—in hindsight—pare back my plans.

*     *     *     *

You see, Tajikistan is largely considered to be the most dangerous—and definitely the poorest—of the 'stans. Following the collapse of the USSR, the country descended rapidly into a civil war that pitted the newly formed government against an unlikely coalition of democratic, Islamic and local ethnic groups. The Russians who still considered the Tajik and Uzbek border to be a part of their own, had kept a military division in place as border guards, which along with Kazakh, Uzbek and Kyrgyz forces proceeded to tacitly support the Tajik government, adding significant firepower to an already violent conflict. With widespread support for the opposition, however, neither side was able to strike a decisive blow, drawing out a bloody war that ultimately led to a stalemate. As a result, 20% of the country's 5.5 million people became internally displaced, and between 60,000 and 100,000 were killed. All of which made this go down as the deadliest conflict within an ex-Soviet state to break out in the wake of the USSR's collapse. With the society, economy and medical system now broken, and after the civil war had finally come to a close, the country was struck by a new calamity as bacteria outbreaks spread across the country with reports of Typhoid and Diphtheria, the latter of which came to be the worst outbreak in the world since The Second World War.

The instability and power vacuum this war created resulted in President Emomali Rahmon, who had held various roles since the Soviet days, 'win' his first and then second election with an unlikely 97% of the vote. Sadly, that same President has continued to 'win' elections and is still in power today, and over the past two decades has systematically destroyed all opposition and has recently begun installing his children into positions of power. And all of this in a country that has a GDP per capita of less than USD$1k, making it the poorest of all the 17 ex-Soviet countries (and indeed one of the poorest countries in the world). So perhaps listening to the bloke I'd met in Kazakhstan or the Australian government's travel advice to "Exercise a high degree of caution" and "Reconsider your need to travel", may have been prudent, but I had a book to write and frankly, my experience in this country proved once more that misconceptions are there to be broken.

# DUSHANBE

Twenty", the guy in the airport had said when I told him the name of my hotel. Having been burnt now several times and having had the foresight to learn what was appropriate, I eventually settled on seven dollars though not without much consternation from him. Which I thought was extremely bloody rich when we arrived three minutes later to the entrance of what turned out to be an airport hotel. Not having the right change, I approached the front desk to break a note, but with the receptionist only being able to break it down to ten dollars and accompanying that by making the point that this should've only cost one dollar, I begrudgingly handed over the money to my driver with its inadvertent tip. Nine extra dollars though was hardly enough to spoil the fact that I found myself staying in an extremely nice hotel, nice enough for a Chinese Government

Delegation who had occupied the entire hotel and was in the process of checking out as I arrived. Another example of Chinese political and financial muscle-flexing itself, another example of a modern communist country mopping up the remnants of an old one.

\*   \*   \*   \*

Dushanbe, home to 800,000 Tajiks and the capital of Tajikistan. A new city built in 1923 in an even newer country created in 1924. 'Dushanbe' meaning 'Monday' deriving from a nearby village's famous fair held annually on a Monday. The fair had been coming to this town for centuries, had been famous across the region, and had seen merchants travelling for days from as far afield as Persia and China. By the time the Bolsheviks arrived in 1920 however, the fair had long since gone, suffocated under the rule of the recent Bukharan Emirs.

By 1922 the Bolsheviks had completed their overthrow of the old regime in Russia and had evolved along with the recently created Socialist Republics in Central Asia and Eastern Europe, into the Union of Soviet Socialist Republics (USSR) otherwise known as the Soviet Union. And with the determination and zeal of the young Tajik Soviets and the resources of this newly formed union, the construction of Dushanbe got underway in earnest with the goal of creating a new modern Soviet styled capital.

This was no easy task however, for Dushanbe was surrounded by little in the way of resource, let alone industry, meaning everything had to be brought in. And being nestled at the base of the Pamir Mountain Range, containing some of the world's tallest peaks all of which had to be crossed, made this nigh impossible. The effort and expense were enormous as captured by Monica Whitlock in her book *Land beyond the River:*

> *Local building materials—mud and straw—were not used. Poplar wood was too soft to support buildings on a grand scale and gnarled juniper was unsuitable. Each pane of glass, each nail, even timber, was procured elsewhere in the Union, packed into trains and freighted often thousands of miles to the railhead at Termez. Here everything was strapped to camels and hauled along the last leg to Dushanbe over roads so rough that each plank reportedly lost a yard in length.*

And if the distance and geography weren't enough, these Soviets had another obstacle to face, one which required the accompaniment of the Red Army Guards, the Basmachi.

\*   \*   \*   \*

Widespread resentment in the region against the Russians had existed since they first started arriving in the 19th century, but had grown particularly pronounced since WW1 following the violent suppression of the Central Asia Rebellion. Despite *those* Russians being overthrown by the Bolsheviks, many across Central Asia simply saw their neighbour to the north as different in name only. So, when the Bolsheviks began arriving and turning the ancient customs of Central Asia on their head, these resentments erupted once again.

With weapons and money being secretly funnelled into the hands of these rebels by the British and the Emir of Bukhara who was now exiled in Afghanistan, this rebellion soon acquired some level of organisation. The term 'Basmachi' was denoted on them by the Bolsheviks and meant bandit, but they were far too organised to be simple thieves. While the Soviets were trying to establish their newest Soviet Socialist Republic, these Basmachi would thwart any effort they could, blowing up bridges, murdering Red Army soldiers and almost at one point turning the tide against them. Alarmed by this sudden turn of events, the Soviets caved to some of the local Tajik's grievances by reducing the tax burden and relaxing their anti-Islamic measures, all the while shipping in more firepower. By 1931 they had captured the Basmachi leader, Ibrahim Bek, and but for a brief resurgence a couple of years later, had more or less ended the movement. It was said that after being captured and sent by plane to Dushanbe, that Bek looked down upon the vast Soviet collective cotton fields, the roads and canals, the machine and tractor stations, and his head dropped. And on landing, it was said he told the Tajik Soviets that "had he known the real extent of Tajikistan's progress... he would never have undertaken the task of starting a counter-revolution". Of course, this being reported by the Soviet authorities at the time almost certainly meant it was questionable. They executed him soon after.

With the Basmachi threat properly subdued, the Soviets were able to focus on the development of Dushanbe and the Tajiks that lived there. While the modern view of the Soviet Union is almost wholly negative, during these early days it was a force for, if not anything else, the development of an extremely undeveloped part of the world. People whose sole method of transport was the donkey were suddenly introduced to the aeroplane. Backbreaking work in fields was almost overnight replaced with tractors. Though perhaps *most* beneficial to the Tajiks were the arrival of Soviet education and medicine.

Prior to the Soviets arriving, a common treatment for ailments had been to swallow pieces of paper with specific verses from the Koran written on them. This would be administered by what some would call a witch doctor, others a Mullah. The same Mullahs that would appear in the madrassahs in which they taught their pupils an Islamic and Koranic centric world view. When an early census was taken, it was shown that the literacy rate amongst Tajiks hovered around 0.5%. By 1939, after less than two decades of Soviet rule, the literacy rate had reached 83%.

For some Tajiks, especially Tajik women, the changes brought about by the Soviets was on the whole good. Though for all Tajiks, the confrontations they were pulled into was bad, and none were so bad as The Great Patriotic War, World War 2.

*    *    *    *

I woke early and pulled apart my curtains to reveal a still sleeping city sitting under a clear morning sky. The city was nestled up against the Fann Mountain range, called by some as the most beautiful in all of Central Asia, and the sun was peering over them, not yet obscured by the haze of pollution that would later appear. Stretching up into those mountains were the reasonably close foothills, which looked to be the ideal spot to start the day from, so putting my runners on, I set out for a jog.

The streets were empty but for the occasional car spluttering by. A few kids dressed in their school gear and accompanied by their parents were wandering to school, all of whom stopped and stared as a white man with a woman's haircut ran past. I ran through the broken back streets of the city as they steadily rose through the foothills before eventually reaching the outer edge of the suburbs and the beginning of a pine forest. A dirt track took me between rows of pines with the steepness of the track and the fragrance of the trees conspiring to remind my lungs that I was a smoker. The track ended at an ornamentally dressed road at the top of the hill, and stopping to catch my breath, I watched as a row of soldiers in single file marched past me. I looked around to see that I'd inadvertently reached a large monument to the Second World War.

It had been built decades earlier as a home to the Victory Day Parades, a Soviet Union-wide exercise that every 9th of May would celebrate Communism's defeat of Nazism. Which of course was something to celebrate, though presumably, this must've been somewhat bittersweet to the Tajiks (and other Central Asians) after being forced to fight a war that wasn't really theirs. For like all of the Central Asia Republics, the Soviets conscripted them into the War on masse. Three hundred thousand Tajiks took part in the Great War, of which almost 100,000 died, a substantial amount in any regard but especially given that Tajikistan's population was only about 1.5 million at the time. Compare that with New Zealand whose population at the time was 2 million yet lost 'only' 12,000 soldiers or Australia which lost 27,000 soldiers from a population of 7 million. It is interesting that following independence in 1992, the Tajikistani government made a concerted effort to remove the Soviet statues from across the country, yet left alone the monuments to the Great War. Even more so when—at least in this instance—they retained the Soviet symbolism, the hammer and sickle and the Soviet Star.

I walked to a vantage point and looked out across Dushanbe. The Fann Mountains sat dominating the view as they towered above the city, climbing ever higher until the greenery gave way to snow, and the distant tops of the mountains disappeared amongst clouds. From the mountains ran two rivers that cut down from their valleys before joining and dissecting Dushanbe in two. Heavily treed streets separated grey practical buildings, most of which were only a few floors high though punctuated by the second tallest flagpole in the world*, its 165 m high 700 kg Tajikistani

---

* This flagpole was the tallest in the world when it was completed in 2011 but was overtaken in 2014 by a flagpole in Jeddah, Saudi Arabia.

flag slowly unfurling in the breeze. And only 60 km beyond Dushanbe sat the border that the Soviets had demarcated with Uzbekistan, an act that "… deprived Tajik people of their historical cultural centres… an act evaluated as a national tragedy". I contemplated, as I jogged back to my hotel, that up here I had stood between two national tragedies, both perpetrated by the Soviets. Perhaps maintaining the Soviet symbolism was as much as a reminder of the perpetrator as it was of the victim.

*   *   *   *

My hotel sat on a long road, connected to what had been known as Lenin Avenue, but since independence, as Rudaki Avenue, named after a Persian poet born in what would be modern Tajikistan. Ornamentally decorated apartment blocks with French-style balconies lined the avenue and peered through tall leafy trees that grew from wide pedestrian sidewalks. Plush government buildings sat adjacent to the apartments, along with a plaza that led to an opera house, and at the street's end the Parliament of Tajikistan. It felt European, more so given that the people didn't share the Mongol and Chinese characteristics like their Kazakh and Kyrgyz neighbours to the north. In fact, if you removed the skull caps known as Tokis from the heads of the men, you'd almost consider them Eastern European, Romanian perhaps. That there were no outward religious displays probably contributed to it. When the city had been built it was to be—so the boast went—the first city in Central

Asia without a mosque. And since independence, particularly following the civil war which had involved an Islamic opposition, the government has actively subdued anything Islamic orientated, including the call to prayer and the hijab, both forbidden. But make no mistake, despite no outward appearance, the country is indeed Islamic and in turn very conservative. One entirely unscientific study I undertook was via tinder. For unlike the other Central Asian countries (but for Turkmenistan which hardly had the internet) there weren't multitudes of women looking for relationships or anything for that matter. In fact, of the presumed 400,000 women in the city, a mere three were using Tinder. All of whom hid their faces and one whose profile had read "Do you like nature and cats? Ready to spend hours discussing Coelho's work with me reading Yesenini's poems to me? So, you're gay and I do not like you". I didn't—sadly—connect with her which was a shame as she sounded just lovely. That Tinder was not being used perhaps had something to do with a Tajik woman's status. While here, I met a Catalan woman named Maria who was working with an EU funded NGO. "Respectful women", Maria said with air quotes, "would not be seen on the streets past 6 or 7 pm. They get married at 20 and become slaves to their husbands". Maria went on to say that over the three months she had worked in Dushanbe, she had been harassed constantly while walking the streets. At first, she had thought this was because she was a foreigner, but no, sighed her colleagues, it was because she was a woman.

\*    \*    \*    \*

I carried on walking the Rudaki Avenue, reaching the end where on one side sat the Parliament of Tajikistan, guarded by police vehicles covered in CCTV cameras with 'China Aid' conspicuously stamped along their sides. And opposite the Parliament, thrusting a golden sceptre into the sky, adorned in a crown and cape, and standing under an arch, itself topped with a large golden crown, stood the statue of Ismail Somoni, the mythologised founder of the Tajik people.

Ismail Somoni had ruled the Samanid Empire at the turn of the 10th century AD. He had been its ruler when it became the first Central Asian empire to break away from the Islamic caliphate that had ruled the region since the Arabs invaded two centuries earlier. His empire extended across all of modern Central Asia and Afghanistan and included parts of Iran and Pakistan. He considered himself and his people to be the descendants of an older pre-Islamic Persian empire and while he continued the practise of Islam, he replaced the Arab culture and language with that of the Persian. Bukhara became the capital of the empire and it was during this time that Bukhara and indeed Central Asia experienced a golden age with the Samanid rulers promoting the arts and sciences. Yet this wasn't to last as Turkic tribes from the north moved in, eventually conquering Bukhara and its surrounds and pushing the remnants of the Samanid Empire east and into modern Tajikistan. But it is for those reasons that the Tajiks unlike the other Central Asia countries, speak a Persian dialect and are referred to as Central Asian Persians, and moreover why their prized founder is buried in a tomb in Bukhara.

\*    \*    \*    \*

Beyond this ancient symbol of the nation stood its modern one, slowly unfurling in the breeze atop a pole the height of a tall building. And sitting between these two symbols of the nation stood the 'Palace of Nations', a large neoclassical building sporting a golden cupola and home to Emomali Rahmon, autocratic ruler of the country. That it dwarfs the nearby building of Parliament neatly illustrates where power in the country truly lies.

And sadly, it doesn't look like that power will disappear anytime soon. In 2016 a referendum was held asking Tajik citizens whether they wanted to amend their constitution and remove Presidential term limits. A difficult to believe 96.6% voted in its favour. Though with such supposed popularity it seems incongruous that Rahmon would need his image adorned frequently across the country. Yet I spotted his image at least once an hour in Dushanbe alone. Either he was a narcissistic show pony (a possibility) or like his surrounding dictator brethren, a cult of personality was seen as essential to a grip on power. And it was interesting to note the stylistic differences between them. Kazakhstan's President would be the image of the technocrat, standing in a suit with his jacket thrown over his shoulder, his achievements in writing. Conversely, rather than listing his achievements (of which there were few) Turkmenistan's President would be astride a horse or holding a puppy, both symbols of the nation. For Rahmon though, he would almost always be crudely photoshopped amongst fields or in front of mountains, images representative of such a beautiful country. For he was—so the imagery suggested—the country itself, and the country him. Which carrying on with the allegory meant that I suppose I wanted to mount Rahmon, for looking around me at the Fann Mountains in the distance I had a desperate urge to climb them.

# ENEMAS AMONGST
# THE MOUNTAINS

'd been eyeing the mountains above the city since the day
I landed and had begun the search for a guide to take me
to them as soon as my phone found WIFI. Two days later
I was sitting in the foyer of my hotel when I met my new
guide, Jamal. But for his Toki hat, it was hard to tell Jamal
apart from any dark-skinned 38-year-old European. And
much like any well-rounded European male, he was as interested in history and politics as he was in alcohol and women.
It was hard not to like him as he explained his fascination
with America, and of the various humorous idiosyncrasies of
each nationality he'd guided to date. And little did I know
that in two days' time he would be receiving an enema from
a mechanical chair, while talking to me as I and a number

of other blokes sat naked in a spa. That though was yet to come as today he'd first be guiding me and two Australian women on a trip to the Romit Nature Reserve.

\*   \*   \*   \*

We headed out of Dushanbe along the Pamir Highway that I had once intended to take all the way to Afghanistan. In his online profile, Jamal had stressed that unlike his brethren he was a sensible driver, something I felt thankful for as beaten up old cars screamed up behind and around us, including one dangerously towing a 4-wheeler quad bike with a bloke sitting on top.

Eventually turning off and onto a dusty road, we passed an old Orthodox Cemetery, a remnant of the pre-Soviet Russian settlers who had been arriving here in the late 19th century. A fast-flowing river ran parallel to us pouring down from the mountains that we were heading into, and feeding the beautiful surrounding landscape, it's vegetation just starting to be brushed by autumn. Sheep dotted the hillsides and occasionally the road, a couple of times stopping us as a flock of them swarmed around our car, pushed on by a Tajik Shepard and a couple of what looked like border collies.

The mountains had closed in on us by the time we stopped, with Jamal parking the car in a clearing and giving us a few hours to explore the valley before we needed to be back for lunch. The women took their books down to the river while I contently set off up the valley.

Small villages sat alongside the river, seemingly empty but for the odd wisp of smoke rising from a chimney. Every so often I would see small figures in the distance attending to a field, who if they saw me would stand and stare back, occasionally offering me a wave. Their intense curiosity suggesting a lack of foreigners.

With less than 30% of the 9 million Tajiks living in urban cities, it was this environment that represented much of Tajikistan. Small villages scattered across vast plains of agriculture and mountain landscapes, probably in somewhat similar circumstances to the environments they found themselves in prior to the Russians arriving. And while walking amongst these pristine mountains, you could be forgiven for thinking this as some idyllic existence, though it was no coincidence that the two poorest Central Asian nations were also the two most rural.

*     *     *     *

I surprised myself that I'd been away so long as my two-hour podcast came to an end, and spotting a bridge over the river, decided I'd attempt to head back along the other side. Though I could see that first meant passing through a village. The village was made up of rudimentarily built stone houses, tightly packed against one another, and separated by dirt tracks. But for the clucking of chickens behind a small wire fence, the village was silent, that was until two small children chasing each other appeared from nowhere stopping dead in their tracks when they found me, their mouths agape. More children appeared, and as if I were the pied piper, a trail of them formed as I walked deeper into their village. They were all curious and sweet, dressed in basic clothing and grinning black toothed smiles. One of the kids had run off and fetched their mother who came out to initially stare at me, her face tanned and weathered, before she began shouting at what I presumed to be questions.

"Can I walk through?" I said to this blank face, pointing to indicate my direction. She disappeared into a house and came back with another couple of adults who began peppering me with foreign words. "Through", I motioned my hands like railway tracks, "Me... Walk... That way", I exclaimed now using my index and middle finger to indicate walking. The crowd continued to grow till what seemed to be the entire village standing around me. "Me", I pointed at my chest, "Walk", I made the walking signal, "Through", showing my direction. More perplexed faces until one, wide-eyed, finger in the air, shouted "Doctor!" I shook my head in shame feeling as if I'd disappointed them. Awkwardly smiling at the crowd, I placed my hand on my heart and bowed before turning and walking away while feeling slightly self-conscious as the entire village watched in silence as I walked back to the bridge.

*   *   *   *

I arrived back in time for lunch, which Jamal had spontaneously arranged with one of the villagers. The patriarch of a small family came out to greet us and led us into the front room of his house, seating us around a low table. Small kids walked in behind him with plates and cutlery followed by their mother carrying a large bowl of soup and vegetables. It was a poor village and in place of meat, bread had been substituted and instead of a broth, there was a creamy goat's milk. A pile of large round bread was placed next to the soup, and Jamal broke this apart into pieces which he handed to us and poured hot tea into soup bowls for us to drink. The food was, despite its simplicity, delicious owing probably to the ingredients coming directly from the surrounding farms.

Both the Australian women turned out to be audiologists from Hobart and were on a voluntary trip to assist with deafness amongst Tajik children that was at rates ten times that of Australia. They had funded this trip through a combination of their own money along with that raised by punters in pub quizzes across Hobart. The high rate of deafness was for two reasons, they explained, the first being the antibiotics prescribed by doctors long since banned in the West, and the second due to genetic defects that came about through the common Tajik practise of marrying your cousin. All of which was a slightly awkward conversation to have next to Jamal who sat in silence and listened.

\*       \*       \*       \*

I waited in the foyer, this time with a bag packed for an overnight stay. We were heading deep into the Fann Mountains today, and I was a little trepidatious as I looked out across the city shrouded in darkness, the sun hidden by heavy clouds.

Jamal arrived, slapped me on the back in greeting and threw my bag in the back of the truck. "How are you feeling today?" Jamal quizzed me, "Kinda constipated actually". "Well you could always try drinking that", Jamal responded with a wink as he pointed to a dirty puddle of water next to the car.

We cut through the city and up into the hills, before the road took on a new steepness as we climbed the mountains, passing small villages in the distance. It was among these villages that lived the last remaining speakers of Yaghnobi, a two and a half thousand-year-old language. And once spoken by the Sogdians, a long since gone people who ruled this area before being destroyed in 330 BC by Alexander the Great and his army. Only twelve and a half thousand Yagnobi speakers exist today, and almost all of them were amongst these mountains.

"It may snow", Jamal said casually as he looked up through the windshield. I had started to wonder the same since the temperature was dropping noticeably, and the diffused light of the sun was getting weaker as the clouds got darker. With these roads being famously dangerous enough, it wasn't a proposition I relished, particularly not as we approached the Anzob Tunnel. This tunnel had been built in 2006, cut 5 km through the Fann Mountains and allowed drivers to avoid bypassing through Uzbekistan. When it was opened, drivers were required to sign a waiver form noting the potential hazards faced inside the tunnel, giving it the nickname the 'Tunnel of Death'. On arriving, I realised it was hardly that, though it was a 5 km long pitch-black unventilated pot-holed tunnel that the dimly glowing orange lights of Jamal's truck had trouble lighting up. Fortunately for us, container trucks were aggressively racing by and lighting it up with their floodlights allowing us to pass through to the other side after an ass clenching 15 minutes.

Exiting out the other side though, we entered into a different world. Sun beamed down from a blue sky onto a dry road, as enormous cathedral-like mountains soared rapidly away from either side of the road. We were already 3,000 m above sea level, and the mountains on either side of us shot up steeply for another kilometre. "That tunnel is why we support Rahmon", Jamal declared referring to the Tajik President. "He builds tunnels and roads throughout the country for us". "Yes, but in our country, we expect our leaders to build them and if they don't, we replace them with someone who does", I hadn't meant to but I suspected that my response had come off rather smug. "Though it should be said, Australia is not a good example of Democracy at the moment. We've had six Prime Ministers in ...". I trailed off. "Well... this fucking government is at least better than an Islamist government", came his reply. If the situation were that binary, then perhaps I'd agree. For much of the 90s, the country had shared a border with the Taliban government to their south, though of course, that threat had now gone. "But they do take everything from us. If you have a good business, the president's relatives will take it", Jamal continued, "there is no future for Tajiks in Tajikistan". It was true, the Tajikistan government is regarded as one of the most corrupt in the world, and indeed many private industries had been captured by his family. The current mayor of Dushanbe is the President's son, and it is assumed that he is being groomed to take over when his father steps down.

*    *    *    *

We turned off the main road and crossing a bridge entered onto an uneven stony road that cut through a valley. Rust coloured mountains soared up on either side of us, and as we followed the river that ran alongside us, we reached a small village made up of 50 or so cottages, surrounded by the area's only trees. The road turned upwards away from the valley, and we climbed over the foot of a mountain before dipping back down with a ravine to our left and what looked like an unstable cliffside to our right. Taking a steep hairpin turn, the view opened up and presented what we'd driven all this way for. Before us lay Lake Iskanderkul, named after Alexander the Great who had passed by this lake almost two and half thousand years earlier. Glaciers high up in the mountains were perpetually grinding away at the mountain rock, creating a fine rock powder that was carried via streams to this lake, colouring it a powdery turquoise. The surrounding snow-peaked mountains reflected along the lake's surface like a mirror, undisturbed by the perfectly still air.

Our stony road took us around the lake's edge and crossed us over a quaint wooden bridge that sat over a stream fed from a spring which bubbled and sparkled in the sun. Jamal parked the car and insisted on us both drinking from the spring which was ice cold but tasted pristine and fresh. "Bucephalus drank from this spring", Jamal explained to me.

My phone suddenly vibrated, and I looked down to see that out here in the middle of a mountain range surrounded by no one, I was picking up 4G reception. Which became less surprising as Jamal pointed out that the single grand house sitting amongst a manicured lawn of trees at the lake's edge, surrounded by a high pointed fence, was the summer house of the President.

The house sat against a hill which, Jamal explained, hemmed in a valley which was home to a tiny village. Having pestered him about doing some semblance of exercise, he agreed to drop me in the valley, allowing me an hour to walk back. We jumped into the car and zig-zagged our way up the hill, before arriving in the clearing of a rather barren valley occupied by a handful of houses amongst fields. I got out of the car which then disappeared back over the hill, taking the only noise in the valley with it.

A man suddenly stood up in a nearby field and stood completely still while staring at me in a perplexed fashion. Had I caught him crapping I wondered. I smiled and waved which startled him, until he waved back, a wide friendly grin appearing across his face, revealing a toothless mouth. I wonder whether he's benefiting from the 4G reception I thought to myself.

I certainly was going to though, and using that reception, I put my headphones on and turned on a podcast, an interview with Bill Gates, who over the course of the next hour of walking expressed what he saw as the key elements required by a country to move from developing to developed status. "Willingness to reduce corruption ... that makes a huge difference", Bill Gates explained to his interviewer Ezra Klein as I eventually walked past the President's summer residence, with a gardener tilling his lawn.

*　　*　　*　　*

We arrived to the accommodation for the night, a large sprawling complex spread across a ridgeline overlooking a valley covered in snow. "You want treatment?" Jamal asked me as I was checking in. "Like spa and health", he followed up on seeing my confused expression.

We deposited our bags in our room and confusingly headed across to a doctor's office. "Any issue? Doctor wants to know", Jamal asked me as I sat opposite the doctor who was dressed in a white robe and had an ancient-looking stethoscope hanging around his neck. "Well... actually, the constipation". "Ah yes" followed by a back and forth conversation between the doctor and Jamal who as part of his gesticulation included making a circle with his index finger and thumb and scrunching it up tightly. The doctor wrote a script, stood up, shook my hand and directed me to the adjacent room where I was told to strip and lay face down on a massage table.

'A massage, ok' I thought followed by 'Christ, is he wearing eyeliner', as I lifted my head to greet my male masseuse. My underwear was swiftly turned into a G-String and so started a vigorous 45-minute massage. "Is good?" Asked Jamal, "yes, but I would prefer a Thai female", "this same as Thai massage?", "Shit, I hope not" I joked though this was lost on him.

With a slap on my back, the masseuse finished up and walked out. I stood up feeling somewhat more limber and looked out at the snow flurries swirling around the window. Jamal motioned for me to follow him, and slipping back on our clothes, we dashed out through the snow and into a new building. This one was simply a long room with beds on either side, separated by curtains, one of which I was directed to and asked to strip. "I don't understand what we're doing Jamal", I said to Jamal who was on the other side of a curtain, "Hot tar, it's good for the digestion", came his confusing response. A male nurse walked in with a blue tarpaulin sheet covered in an inch-thick layer of black petroleum jelly and lay it on the bed before indicating for me to lie down and place my buttocks directly onto the jelly. *OOooo hot*, I thought as the wax squelched its way around and between my ass, before the nurse now wearing gloves grabbed my penis and balls and moved them out of the way in order to get the wax up between my legs. He left before returning with a new sheet of wax which he placed on top and thereby encompassing my whole waist in the steaming petroleum. I lay back and stared out the window in an infinite amount of confusion. The curtain next to me was suddenly yanked back by Jamal who giving me a big thumbs up revealed that he too was nude but for a petroleum nappy. Half an hour passed as I lay there looking out across the now completely white valley as petroleum fumes rose from my nappy, my downstairs slowly cooking.

"Ok now we have spa", finally I thought, something normal. "We add Radon to it—good for throat". Radon, the radioactive substance that if you do a quick google search will tell you is the second cause of lung cancer after smoking. We walked into the room where three old men sat around a deep steaming plunge pool, all of whom stared as I dipped myself in with them. I said hello and they nodded back, but it didn't seem like the place to engage everyone in deep discussion. "Here, doctor wants you to sit on this", which was a seat in the corner of the room that shot water gently up your ass. "I'm ok, thanks". 'Ok' shrugged my driver as he went and placed his bare ass on it and turned up the tap. I lay there in this spa, looked around at the old nude men sitting by themselves in silence, my nude driver three feet away, head in hands, quietly receiving an enema, and as the warm radon infused steam gently wafted around the room and the snow drifted past the window, I lay back, content, and thought... "Fuck this will be good for my book".

# EPILOGUE

had set out to find the unusual and had ended my trip naked with a group of old men, breathing in radon infused steam. They were Tajik men, looking like Eastern Europeans and speaking a dialect of Persian. So different from their Central Asian brethren to the north, the Kyrgyz and Kazakhs whose round faces, and narrow eyes belied their relationships with the Mongols and Chinese. And sitting amongst snow-covered peaks, some of the world's tallest, vastly different to the Turkmens to the West, who's culture had grown up and adapted to the confines of a desert. The Uzbeks were perhaps most closely linked to the Tajiks with their respective histories overlapping the other's, but it wasn't hard to spot the difference in appearance and temperament between these two cultures.

For a region that is often regarded as one homogenous group, it proved to be anything but. For a moment in history, it had been united, first as Turkestan under the Romanovs, and then in communist solidarity under the Soviets. For all else, it had been an area of different people jostling against one another, being shaped by surrounding forces greater than them. Much like the situation it finds itself in today.

Yet, Central Asians were not always the bit players of history, and at times burst forth upon the world spreading science, ideas and often a blood-soaked sword. As the world circles back towards a point it had been many times in the past, what does the world hold for Central Asia, and Central Asia for the world.